THE FOURMILE WASH PROJECT

ARCHAEOLOGICAL INVESTIGATIONS AT EIGHT SITES IN THE TONOPAH AREA IN WESTERN ARIZONA

by

EARL W. SIRES

With contributions by

SUZANNE K. FISH
GARY FUNKHOUSER
BRUCE B. HUCKELL
LISA W. HUCKELL
LINDA J. PIERCE
ARTHUR W. VOKES

SWCA, INC.
Environmental Consultants
Flagstaff and Tucson

SWCA ANTHROPOLOGICAL RESEARCH PAPER NUMBER 1

1992

ISBN 1 – 931901 – 00 – 7

TABLE OF CONTENTS

LIST OF FIGURES

LIST OF TABLES

FOREWORD

SWCA, Inc., an environmental consulting firm, in late 1987 expanded its capabilities by offering archaeological consulting services as well. The firm was founded in 1981 with a commitment to providing responsible services concerning today's complex environmental problems. This philosophy was extended to the variety of archaeological services that SWCA provides today. As part of the services of SWCA and as a commitment to publishing the results of archaeological investigations for the archaeological community, we have implemented a publication series that is designed to provide thorough reporting of significant research projects. This volume is the first in the series, and we are proud to make it available to all interested institutions and individuals.

SWCA has engaged Robert C. Euler as the general series editor, Richard V. N. Ahlstrom as assistant editor, and Sally P. Bennett as copy editor.

The Fourmile Wash Project presents the results of investigations at eight sites in the Tonopah Desert, an area that until recently received little attention. The resources of the area have drawn little interest due to the general character of the sites and the small number of cultural resource management projects in the western desert of Arizona. The growing data base for the area is the result of the ongoing management practices of the Bureau of Land Management, the development of the Central Arizona Project by the Bureau of Reclamation, and the construction of the Palo Verde nuclear plant and its associated features. The Fourmile Wash Project contributes in a small way to the existing data base but has provided significant insights into land-use strategies in the Tonopah Desert.

Steven W. Carothers
President, SWCA, Inc.

ABSTRACT

The Fourmile Wash Data Recovery Project (SWCA Project No. 22-88160-1) included excavation and other data recovery activities at eight archaeological sites located in northwestern Maricopa County, Arizona. The excavations were conducted between 18 April and 5 May 1988 by SWCA, Inc., under contract with Headquarters West, Ltd. The project was necessitated by the fact that these sites are located on lands administered by the U.S. Bureau of Land Management (BLM) that were scheduled to be transferred to private ownership as part of a land exchange. The project sites are located 42 miles west of Phoenix, Arizona, in northwestern Maricopa County, northeast of Tonopah, Arizona. They are situated along a three-mile stretch of Fourmile Wash within T.3N, R.6W, sec. 34, NE¼NE¼ and sec. 35, W½, and T.2N, R.6W, sec. 10 (USGS 15 minute, Belmont Mountains Quadrangle).

The project sites were first identified during the Lower Gila–White Tanks West Project (BLM-020-10-88-202), a pedestrian survey of 8,960 acres conducted by BLM personnel from the Phoenix District Office. The purpose of the project was to gather and interpret information regarding the prehistoric occupations represented by these sites and to mitigate the potential adverse impact of future actions upon these sites.

Initially, investigators determined that the project sites had been occupied primarily between A.D. 900 and 1150. However, the area was occupied at least as late as A.D. 1400. The eight sites represent loci utilized in a variety of subsistence activities during the seasonal round of a local population, including the gathering of wild plant resources and the hunting of game animals. In addition, researchers determined that the occupants may have cultivated maize and chenopods using floodwater farming techniques. The populations that had inhabited the region had perhaps been local groups distinct from surrounding groups such as the Hohokam. The ceramic assemblage and other aspects of the artifact assemblage indicated that these local populations had interacted with neighboring culture groups.

PROJECT BACKGROUND

Between 18 April and 5 May 1988, SWCA conducted a data recovery program at eight sites in northwestern Maricopa County, Arizona (SWCA Project No. 22-88160-1). This project was conducted under contract with Headquarters West, Ltd., and required 105-person-field days to complete.

The project sites were first identified during the Lower Gila-White Tanks West Project (BLM-020-10-88-202), an intensive pedestrian survey of 8,960 acres conducted by Bureau of Land Management (BLM) personnel from the Phoenix District Office (Stone 1988). This survey was conducted in anticipation of a now-completed land exchange involving BLM lands west of Phoenix and private lands southeast of Tucson. Fifty-one sites were discovered and recorded during the survey, twenty-nine of which are located along Fourmile Wash. Thus, approximately 57% of the sites are located in an area that constitutes only 14% of the area surveyed. The sites are identified by their Arizona State Museum (ASM) site numbers, which are correlated with their BLM site numbers in the following list:

ASM No.	BLM No.
AZ T:5:8	AZ T:5:21
AZ T:5:9	AZ T:5:19
AZ T:5:10	AZ T:5:20
AZ T:5:11	AZ T:5:11
AZ T:5:12	AZ T:5:12
AZ T:5:14	AZ T:5:14
AZ T:5:16	AZ T:5:16
AZ T:5:17	AZ T:5:51

LOCATION

The project area is located 42 miles (68 km) west of Phoenix, Arizona, in northwestern Maricopa County (Figure 1.1). The town of Tonopah is located 7 miles (11 km) to the southwest. Specifically, the project area is located within T.3N, R.6W, sec. 34, NE¼NE¼ and sec. 35, W½, and T.2N, R.6W, sec. 10, E½, SE¼NW¼, NE¼SW¼ (USGS 15 minute, Belmont Mountains Quadrangle).

PHYSIOGRAPHY

The project area is situated in the Sonoran Desert subdivision of the basin and range physiographic province, which is characterized by northwest-southeast-trending mountain ranges separated by broad, flat alluvial valleys. The eight project sites lie within the Tonopah Desert, a level valley floor dissected by numerous south-trending washes (Figure 1.2). Elevation within the project area ranges between 1,180 feet and 1,280 feet above sea level. The Belmont Mountains are located 3 miles (5 km) to the north. Other major geological structures in the region include the White Tank Mountains to the east, the Big Horn Mountains to the west, and the Palo Verde Hills to the south. Locally prominent geological features include Hot Rock Mountain and Flatiron Mountain, isolated volcanic hills located just to the northwest and north of the project area. Chapter 6 contains a detailed discussion of the geomorphology of the project area.

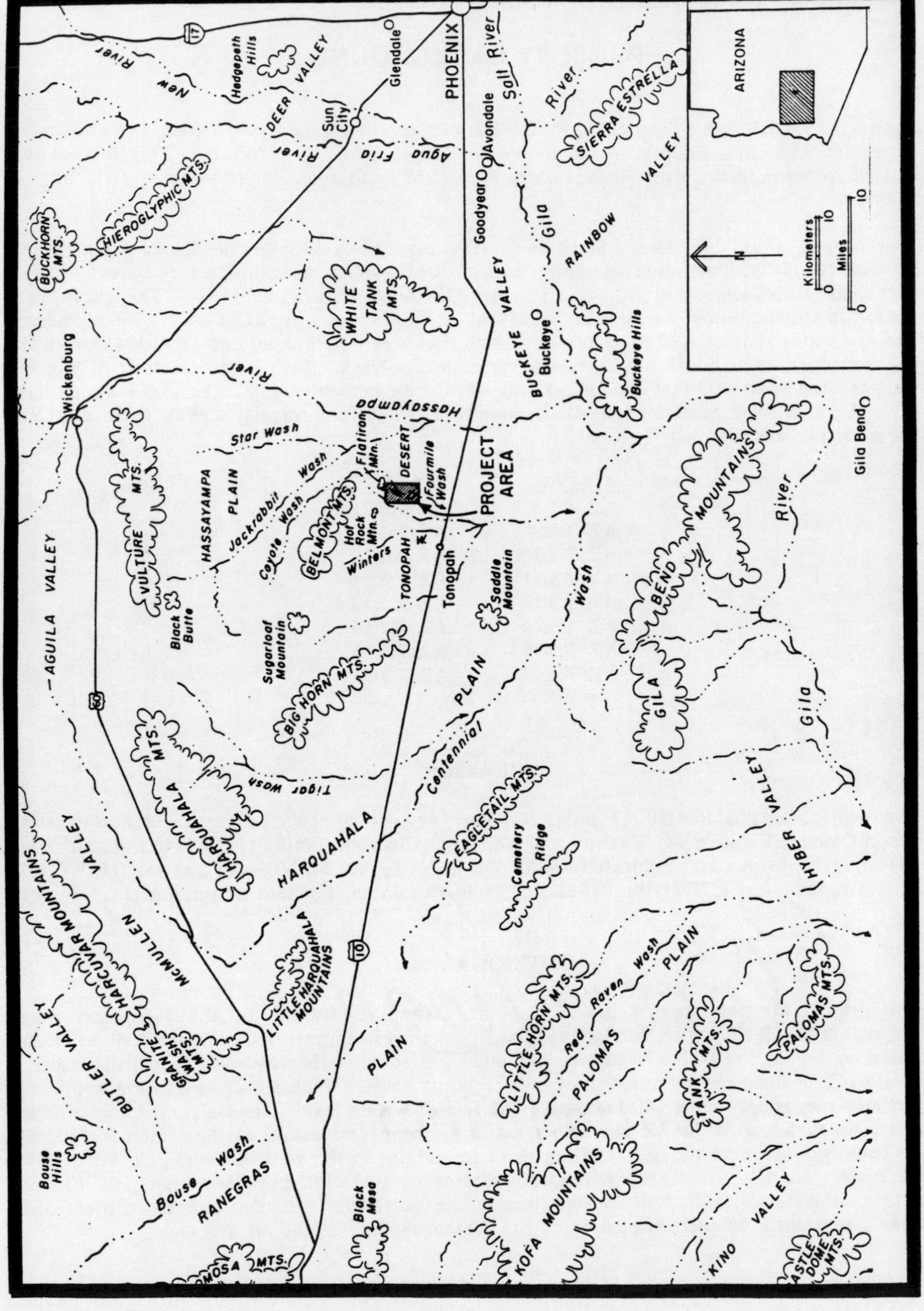

Figure 1.1. Location of Fourmile Wash Project area.

Western Arizona is included within the southwestern Colorado River watershed. The primary drainage in the project vicinity is the Hassayampa River, located 6 miles (10 km) to the east. The Hassayampa, a major drainage in western Arizona, rises in the mountains south of Prescott. Among the more substantial washes in the area are Old Camp Wash, Winters Wash, Jackrabbit Wash, and Fourmile Wash, all of which eventually drain into the Gila River less than 20 miles (32 km) to the south.

CLIMATE

As might be expected, the Tonopah Desert is an area of extreme heat and low rainfall. Average monthly temperatures for July and August exceed 90°F, and the temperature is greater than 90°F an average of 168 days per year. The frost-free period averages 329 days per year. Annual rainfall averages eight inches, most of which (42%) occurs during frontal winter storms between December and March. Cyclonic summer storms during July and August add an additional 27% of the annual rainfall. The spring and fall months are generally exceedingly dry.

FLORA AND FAUNA

The project area is located in the creosote-bursage (Lower Colorado Valley) series of the Sonoran desertscrub biome (Brown and Stone 1982). Three plant associations have been identified within the study area: the creosote-bursage (*Larrea-Ambrosia*) association, the foothills palo verde–mesquite-ironwood (*Cercidium-Prosopis-Olneya*) association, and the foothills palo verde–saguaro association (*Cercidium-Carnegiea*).

Creosote-bursage associations are found on the level interdrainage areas and are characterized by the presence of sparse creosote bush (*Larrea tridentata*) and occasional bursage (*Ambrosia deltoidea*). Where this community borders the numerous ephemeral drainages, creosote densities increase markedly. Other species noted include infrequent small mesquite (*Prosopis juliflora*), saguaro (*Carnegiea gigantea*), fish-hook barrel cactus (*Ferocactus wislizenii*), and a groundcover of sparse grasses and annuals (*Schismus* spp.).

The palo verde–mesquite-ironwood association is the desert riparian community associated with the more substantial washes of the area. Increased moisture within the washes has resulted in a dense growth of vegetation that includes such species as ironwood (*Olneya tesota*), mesquite, palo verde (*Cercidium* sp.), catclaw (*Acacia greggii*), and hackberry (*Celtis pallida*). In several areas, geomorphological processes have led to the formation of relatively extensive oases containing a variety of trees.

The palo verde–saguaro association on the slopes of the surrounding hills includes cholla and prickly pear cacti (*Opuntia* sp.), barrel cactus, and ocotillo (*Fouquieria splendens*), in addition to the two major species.

Animal species typically found in the area include mule deer (*Odocoileus hemionus*), jackrabbit (*Lepus* sp.), and cottontail (*Sylvilagus* sp.). Bighorn sheep (*Ovis canadensis*) are known from some of the more rugged mountain ranges west of the project area. A variety of species typical of the Sonoran Desert, including coyote (*Canis latrans*), quail (*Lophortyx* sp.), mourning dove (*Zenaida macroura*), roadrunner (*Geococcyx californianus*), red-tailed hawk (*Buteo borealis*), rattlesnake (*Crotalus* sp.), and horned toad (*Phrynosoma* sp.), also inhabit the area.

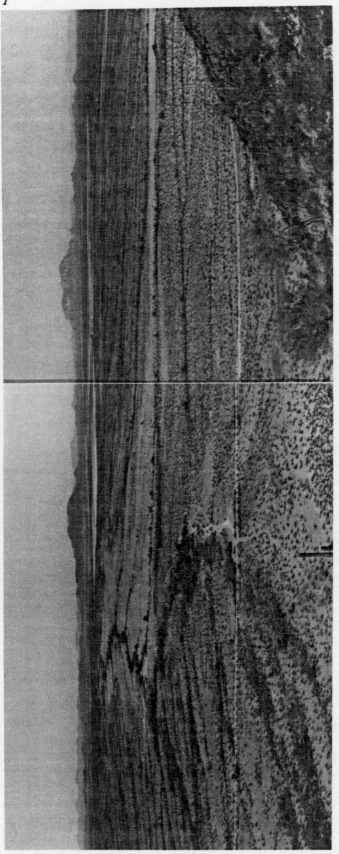

Figure 1.2.   Overview of project area looking south from Flatiron Mountain.

RESEARCH DESIGN AND PROBLEM DOMAINS

Despite the fact that the eight sites investigated during the Fourmile Wash Project were originally identified as discrete entities, their individual characteristics and relative distribution indicate that they should appropriately be treated as members of a single site complex. The sites under consideration form a more or less continuous distribution along 2.5 miles (4 km) of Fourmile Wash (Figure 2.1). Moving from north to south, the distribution of sites begins in the northwestern quarter of T.3N, R.6W, sec. 35 and extends into the southwestern quarter of that same section, as well as into the northwestern corner of T.2N, R.6W, sec. 2. The extent and continuity of the distribution through T.2N, R.6W, sec. 3 is uncertain, since this section is privately owned and was not surveyed, but seven sites were recorded along the wash in T.2N, R.6W, sec. 10. The areal distribution in Figure 2.1 suggests that the cultural remains continue through Section 3.

Based on the results of the survey, investigators determined that the "Fourmile Wash area contained information important to understanding the use of the western Arizona desert by prehistoric Hohokam and Patayan groups" (Stone 1988:45). The BLM subsequently recommended that a data recovery program be conducted, and SWCA prepared a research design (Sires and Gregory 1988:12–15). Much of the following discussion was taken from that document.

SWCA selected the eight sites examined during data recovery because (1) they were representative of the site variability encountered during the survey, (2) they were associated spatially with one another and with Fourmile Wash, and (3) in the case of AZ T:5:12(ASM), also known as the Flatiron Site, the site's size and the presence of at least two subsurface features indicated the possibility that additional subsurface features might be present. The research design was created to maximize the interpretive potential of the information collected during the data recovery program. Based on the characteristics of the sites under consideration and the known prehistory of the area, researchers identified four major problem domains: site function, temporal and cultural affiliation, environment and subsistence, and population size and organization. Each problem domain is discussed below, with specific research questions posed within each domain, followed by a definition of the data required to answer the questions.

SITE FUNCTION

The data recovery program had as its primary goal the definition of site function, to offer explanations for the presence of prehistoric groups within the project area and to clarify the nature of activities conducted by inhabitants of the area. The presence of roasting pits and clusters of various kinds of artifacts, including ground stone, suggested that resource procurement and processing had been important. The data recovery program was also expected to further specify the range of activities that had produced these features and artifact assemblages and to determine what role they had played in the use or occupation of the area. Toward that end, the following specific questions were posed:

1. What activities are represented by the cultural materials and features at the various sites?

2. Were all the sites produced by similar activities?

3. What may be said about the intensity and duration of site use?

4. Can intrasite activity areas be identified?

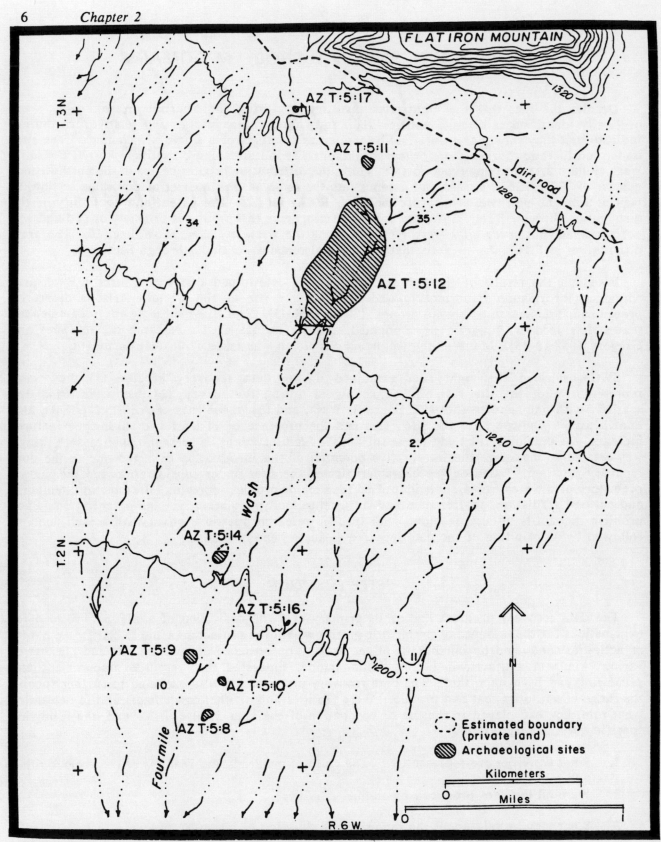

Figure 2.1. Location of Fourmile Wash Project sites.

5. Is there evidence for change in site function through time?

6. Beyond the differing ceramic traditions represented, is there evidence for differential use of the sites by peoples representing different cultural traditions?

To answer these questions, specific kinds of data were required. Analysis of lithic and ground stone tools yielded information on the kinds of activities conducted at the sites. The form and number of ceramic vessels present were important in determining site function and in inferring the intensity and duration of occupation. In addition, the kinds of cultural features present provided information on site function and occupation, and archaeobotanical and faunal remains also were informative in this regard.

The presence of occupation surfaces at two sites suggested a more complex site function and occupational history than at other project sites. Researchers anticipated that artifact diversity would also correlate with functional diversity and probably occupational intensity. All the data classes described above were combined with chronometric data and cultural diagnostics to determine whether use of the project area had changed through time or varied by cultural group.

TEMPORAL AND CULTURAL AFFILIATION

A definition of the temporal and cultural affiliations of the groups involved is basic to an understanding of prehistoric occupation in the project area. Other research in the area has documented the co-occurrence of Lower Colorado Buff Ware and Hohokam ceramics at a number of sites (Brown and Stone 1982; Stein 1981). This pattern also existed at the project sites.

As Stone (1986) notes, this pattern suggests that the area was a frontier zone between the two groups, but the details are not well understood. Do these sites represent mixed temporal assemblages resulting from sequential use of the area, actual social interaction, or simply contact through trade? Once the temporal and cultural affiliations of the various project sites were better understood, it was possible to relate the data from project sites to other research issues of a wider nature and, in turn, apply comparative data to a discussion of project sites. The following questions were considered relevant to these issues:

1. What periods of occupation are represented at the sites?

2. Can the cultural affiliation of the site occupants be established?

3. Are multiple temporal or cultural components present at any of the sites?

4. Is there temporal variability in the use of the area by particular cultural groups?

To answer these questions, investigators examined temporally and culturally diagnostic artifact types such as ceramics and stone tools and sought to establish absolute dates through radiocarbon analysis. After researchers had gained a sense of the chronological and cultural placement of the sites, they used data relating to site function to examine questions about changes in the use of the area through time, use of the area by different cultural groups, and the relationships among various groups that occupied the area. Horizontal stratigraphy was used to determine whether multiple components were present at particular sites.

ENVIRONMENT AND SUBSISTENCE

Relatively large village sites are known to the east of the project area in the White Tank Mountains (Johnson 1963) and to the south along the Gila River (Wasley and Johnson 1965). The intervening desert areas seem to be typified by the presence of smaller, limited-activity sites. Riverine groups routinely traveled over 50 miles (80 km) into the desert to particularly advantageous resource areas (Castetter and Bell 1951; Rogers n.d.). In addition, the possibility that agriculture of some form was practiced along washes cannot be discounted. To address these issues, researchers defined the full range of subsistence activities conducted at the sites and described the nature of the prehistoric environment within which these activities had taken place. The following questions were addressed:

1. What plant, animal, or other natural resources were exploited at the sites within the project area?

2. Are domesticated plant species represented in the archaeological record, or are the remains restricted to wild resources?

3. How were these resources processed and for what purpose? Were surpluses produced, or was the focus on immediate subsistence needs?

4. What can be determined regarding the nature of the prehistoric environment? What aspects of that environment may have been factors in prehistoric occupation?

5. What is the significance of the lushly vegetated areas along Fourmile Wash and its tributaries? What geomorphological conditions are responsible for this pattern? Can these factors be related to the aboriginal use of the area?

Ethnobotanical, faunal, and pollen remains were of primary importance in answering these questions. The presence of plant and animal remains in relevant archaeological contexts such as hearths or roasting pits indicated which species had been important in the prehistoric diet. In addition, the functional analysis of lithic artifacts and analysis of the size and form of ceramic vessels provided insight into how various resources were processed. Ethnobotanical samples and geomorphological analysis provided data regarding the prehistoric environment.

POPULATION SIZE AND ORGANIZATION

The basic distributional pattern of archaeological features at the project sites seemed to be single or clustered roasting pits associated with artifact scatters. In some areas, these scatters were composed of particular artifact types such as ground stone or a number of ceramic vessels and may have represented specialized activity areas. Occupation surfaces were present at AZ T:5:12(ASM) and AZ T:5:17(ASM). An examination of the patterns in the distribution of these features and the relationships between them allowed inferences regarding the size and character of the social groups that had used or occupied the sites. This information influenced the interpretation of issues related to site function, subsistence, and cultural interaction. Several specific research questions were considered relevant to these issues:

1. What is the pattern of distribution of surface features? Are such features spatially clustered or randomly distributed?

2. Is the distribution of artifacts positively correlated with the distribution of features? Are there patterns in the overall distribution of features and artifacts?

3. What may be inferred about the size and composition of the social groups that used or occupied the sites? Were entire social units such as nuclear or extended families present, or was use of the area characterized by the presence of task groups organized for the specific activities conducted there?

4. Do patterns of social organization vary temporally or culturally?

The data used to address these questions included artifact assemblages as well as distributional data such as spatial relationships between features and artifact clusters that might represent work areas. Definition of similar sets of features or artifacts resulted in identification of the spatial domains of particular social groups.

CULTURE HISTORY

The culture history of the project area includes four major periods: Paleoindian, Archaic, Ceramic, and Historic. Table 3.1 presents chronological sequences for western Arizona.

PALEOINDIAN PERIOD

Though arguments exist concerning the earliest arrival of human beings in the New World (Davis et al. 1980; Hayden 1976; Haynes 1980), archaeologists generally agree that by 10,000 B.C. this important population movement had occurred. A moister climate than at present encouraged a more luxuriant vegetational regime, which in turn supported large game such as mammoth and bison. The Paleoindian period lasted until about 8000 B.C. and has been characterized as a pattern of small nomadic bands relying on the pursuit and capture of big game. The primary diagnostic artifacts are lanceolate, fluted projectile points sometimes found in association with the remains of extinct megafauna.

To date, no Paleoindian materials have been identified in western Arizona. This may well be a result of the limited amount of archaeological investigation conducted in the area, thus leaving open the question of early human presence. Traditional views have been questioned recently on the basis of evidence suggesting that populations engaging in other subsistence activities may have been equally important and of comparable antiquity (McGuire and Schiffer 1982; Martin and Plog 1973). Lacking the diagnostic lithic assemblages associated with big-game hunters, however, the residues of these populations may not be as readily recognized and identified.

Researchers have proposed several co-traditions for the Paleoindian period. These include the Clovis/Folsom tradition, which encompasses much of the western United States, and the San Dieguito tradition. The latter is particularly relevant to the present discussion, because it is generally presumed to have incorporated western Arizona (Rogers 1966). Three phases have been defined: San Dieguito I, II, and III (Rogers 1958).

Differences in the composition of the lithic assemblages and the kinds of features present at the largely surficial sites distinguished these phases. Based on correlations with materials from Ventana Cave, San Dieguito I is thought to predate 9000 B.C. San Dieguito III has been placed between 7000 and 6000 B.C. on the basis of radiocarbon dates (Warren 1967). Several researchers have questioned the validity of the San Dieguito concept (Irwin-Williams 1979; McGuire and Schiffer 1982; Warren 1967), but lack of research in the area has prohibited the development of useful alternative models (Gregory 1987).

ARCHAIC PERIOD

Several culture concepts are relevant to an interpretation of the Archaic period in western Arizona, including the Desert (Jennings 1957), Picosa (Irwin-Williams 1967), Amargosa (Rogers 1958, 1966), and Cochise cultures (Sayles and Antevs 1941). The Desert and Picosa culture concepts define the development of a generalized hunting-and-gathering adaptation thought to be typical of Archaic groups throughout the Southwest. The Amargosa concept interprets the Archaic period as representing the displacement or absorption of San Dieguito populations by later groups. The Cochise culture, as originally presented, was divided into three phases based on changes in the artifact assemblages.

Table 3.1. Chronological Sequences for Western Arizona

Patayan		Hohokam	
Waters 1982	Schroeder 1979	Haury 1976	McGuire & Schiffer 1982
Patayan III A.D. 1500+	Yumans A.D. 1500+	Pima/Papago* A.D. 1450+	Pima/Papago* A.D. 1450+
			Classic Period A.D. 1200–1450
Patayan II A.D. 1000–1500	Hakataya	Classic Period A.D. 1100–1450	
			Sedentary Period A.D. 1000–1200
Patayan I A.D. 700–1000	Hakataya	Sedentary Period A.D. 900–1100	
			Colonial Period A.D. 800–1000
		Colonial Period A.D. 550–900	
			Pioneer Period A.D. 500–800
Basket Maker III A.D. 1–300–A.D. 700		Pioneer Period 300 B.C.-A.D. 500	

Late Archaic:	1500 B.C.-A.D. 1–500
Middle Archaic:	4800 B.C.–1500 B.C.
Early Archaic:	8500-6000 B.C-4800 B.C.
Paleoindian, San Dieguito:	9500 B.C.-8500-6000 B.C.

(After Stone 1986:70)

* The Papago are now referred to as the Tohono O'odham.

Continuous and vigorous debate has surrounded all these cultural sequences, especially concerning the validity of the various phase designations and the dating of the phases (Huckell 1984; Irwin-Williams 1979; Whalen 1971). Using more recent data, Huckell (1984) has attempted to clarify this situation by proposing a three-phase division of the Archaic period with date ranges based on changes in projectile point styles. In this model, the early Archaic is defined by points with tapering stems and is dated from 8500 to 4800 B.C. The middle Archaic, 4800 to 1500 B.C., is characterized by Pinto and Gypsum-style points, and the late Archaic period is defined by the presence of San Pedro, Elko corner-notched, Cienega, and concave-based triangular points and dates from 1500 B.C. to A.D. 300 (Huckell 1984).

CERAMIC PERIOD

The Ceramic period has been variously dated for this area from 300 B.C. (Haury 1976) to post–A.D. 1500 (Schroeder 1979; Waters 1982). A number of Ceramic period cultural manifestations have been identified in the area of concern, including Patayan, Hakataya, and Hohokam.

Patayan

The Lowland Patayan ceramic tradition is characterized by the presence of Lower Colorado Buff Ware, thought to have been associated with a group of people inhabiting an area along the Colorado River from Nevada to the Gulf of California and extending up the lower Gila River. Rogers (1945) developed the first chronology for the Patayan culture, proposing three distinct prehistoric periods. These periods are still in use, somewhat modified by subsequent research (McGuire and Schiffer 1982; Waters 1982). Characteristic traits associated with Patayan I (A.D. 700–1000) ceramics include red clay slips, lug and loop handles, rim notching, the Colorado shoulder, burnishing, and incised decoration (Waters 1982).

After A.D. 1000, new ceramic attributes appeared, and existing ones waned. The Colorado shoulder was lost, as were red slips, incising, and burnishing. A number of vessel forms were also discarded. Recurved rims, stucco finishes, and a number of new vessel forms characterized the Patayan II period. Intrusive Patayan sherds at Hohokam sites near Gila Bend led to the suggestion that contact increased between the two groups during this time (Wasley and Johnson 1965). The post–A.D. 1500 Patayan III period includes the Protohistoric and Historic periods in western Arizona. Refinement and continuation of existing attributes such as construction, symmetry, and surface treatment mark this period, not the appearance of new ceramic traits.

Existing models of Patayan subsistence have been based on ethnographic analogy. Similarities in material culture and settlement pattern have led researchers to propose continuity between Patayan and historic Yuman groups (Huckell 1979; McGuire and Schiffer 1982). These groups apparently relied on riverine floodwater farming, fishing, hunting, and gathering as their basic subsistence strategy. According to Swarthout (1981:66), winter base camps were located along the lower foothills east of the Colorado River. The importance of desert resources has been described, with temporary sites away from the river interpreted as representing foraging trips to obtain nonriverine resources (Rogers n.d.).

Hakataya

Schroeder (1957, 1979) has called the indigenous descendants of Archaic groups in central and western Arizona the Hakataya and includes within this concept such diverse groups as the Patayan, Pioneer Hohokam, Salado, Sinagua, and the historic Yumans. According to Schroeder (1957), Hakataya remains are characterized by plain brown and gray ceramics, chopping tools, slab metates, stone and wooden mortars, triangular projectile points, oval or circular brush structures, roasting pits, and insubstantial refuse deposits. Hunting and gathering were important subsistence endeavors, with limited farming practiced in particularly favorable areas. This view of cultural developments in west-central Arizona has been challenged by McGuire and Schiffer (1982). They question the interpretive utility of the concept, given what they consider the overly general criteria employed.

Hohokam

The project area lies to the north and west of the core area of the Hohokam. The presence of Hohokam sherds in low frequencies at sites throughout the western desert attests to their influence, if not their presence, in the region. The Hohokam chronological sequence, lengthy and complex, has generated continuing debate on many related issues. Several reports, including those by McGuire and Schiffer (1982) and Doyel and Plog (1980), offer a more detailed synthesis of this sequence.

Archaeologists generally agree that during much of the sequence the Hohokam were settled in large riverine villages and used extensive canal systems to irrigate a variety of crops. As Stone (1986:69) notes, "wide ranging trade networks, monumental architecture, and the maintenance and management of canal systems suggest organizational and political complexity exceeding that of historic Indian groups." Recent studies have shown that relatively large settlements were also located in a variety of nonriverine locales where alternative forms of agriculture were practiced. In addition, numerous studies of Hohokam small and limited-activity sites have documented a range of exploitive activities in interdrainage areas.

HISTORIC ABORIGINAL PERIOD

The project area falls within the aboriginal range of the Yavapai tribe. Historically, this group was composed of three subtribes, each encompassing several bands (Gifford 1936; Mariella and Khera 1983). These subgroups were distinguished by minor variations in the dialect of the Yuman language that they spoke and by differences in subsistence practices, the latter influenced primarily by local environmental variables.

The highly mobile Yavapai followed an annual cycle of wild resource exploitation, supplementing their diet with small-scale agriculture. According to Mariella (1983), desert bands such as the Wiltaikapaya, who inhabited the region encompassing the project area, relied on mesquite and palo verde beans and saguaro and cholla fruit during the summer. In the fall, they most likely moved to higher elevations to gather piñon nuts, acorns, agave hearts, prickly pear fruits, and walnuts. Meat sources included deer, sheep, rabbits, wood rats, and a variety of amphibians.

The cultivation of corn, beans, squash, and melons complemented the gathering of wild foods. The Yavapai typically planted crops in particularly moist areas, then continued the gathering cycle, only to return some months later for harvesting. Small groups consisting of as many as 10 nuclear or extended families (Gifford 1936:297) occupied a succession of temporary or seasonal base camps.

HISTORIC ANGLO PERIOD

Anglo use of the Tonopah Desert, primarily by early miners and explorers, followed the discovery of rich ore deposits in the nearby mountains sometime after 1864. Supplying the mining camps, a primary concern and a lucrative endeavor, resulted in the construction of roads and the drilling of wells for water. Soon after, the western desert was used for livestock grazing, and ranching continues to be economically important in the project area. Attempts at establishing agricultural communities became reality during the 1920s and 1930s as a result of changes in homesteading laws and the promotion of the area by local communities. Homesteading in these dry and marginally productive areas became a popular alternative to unemployment during the Great Depression (Stein 1981), when towns such as Palo Verde and Wintersburg came into being.

PREVIOUS RESEARCH IN THE PROJECT AREA

Relatively little scientific investigation has been focused on the cultural resources in this portion of the Southwest. Consequently, they are considerably less well known than are those in neighboring areas. Stone's (1986) extensive review of the work that has been conducted should be consulted by anyone wishing additional information about the area.

The larger area of particular interest to the present study is west of Phoenix, Arizona, in a triangle bounded by the Belmont Mountains to the north, the White Tank Mountains to the east, and the Palo Verde Hills and Saddle Mountains to the south. Several archaeological studies have been conducted on the periphery of this area and provide useful comparative data.

Forty-six sites were reported as a part of the study associated with the construction of the Granite Reef Aqueduct of the Central Arizona Project, which passes to the northwest of the project area (Brown and Stone 1982). These sites included artifact concentrations of variable extent and density, trails, rock rings, and food-processing loci. According to Brown and Stone (1982:55), "these temporary camps and activity areas had little depth and the overall pattern of land use was one of travel and temporary, but repeated, utilization of lithic and wild food resources. Diagnostic ceramics and lithics indicated occupation by Archaic, Patayan, and Hohokam groups."

To the southwest of the project area, studies have been conducted in association with the construction of the Palo Verde Nuclear Generation Plant (Fuller 1973; Haas 1973; Stein 1976, 1981; Trott 1974). The Museum of Northern Arizona conducted a survey of 6 square miles (15.6 km²) in 1974 and recorded 35 prehistoric sites. Site types identified included sherd and lithic scatters situated near the larger washes, intaglios, rock rings, rock alignments, petroglyphs, and trails. Both Hohokam and Patayan ceramics were often present. Stein (1976, 1981) excavated 8 of these sites in 1975, and she interpreted them as representing the exploitation of a variety of wild plant and animal resources by both Hohokam and Patayan groups. It was also suggested that ceremonial activities had taken place in the Palo Verde Hills.

Subsequent work included survey and data recovery along the transmission-line route from Palo Verde to Devers, California, conducted by WESTEC Services, Inc. These projects located and recorded 43 sites consisting of rock rings and lithic scatters (Carrico and Quillen 1982). As part of the Navajo-Hopi Relocation Project, the BLM surveyed 7,000 acres within several parcels located between the Hassayampa River and the White Tank Mountains and recorded 3 artifact scatters with associated rock rings and 57 small sites or isolates. The latter category included small clusters of sherds, flaked stone, ground stone, and rock features. In general, the materials recorded during the survey tended to cluster near the bases of mountains and washes.

Northland Research conducted an archaeological survey in the Harquahala Valley Irrigation District approximately 25 miles (40 km) west of the project area along Centennial Wash (Bostwick 1984, 1988). Further investigations at 8 sites dating primarily to the Archaic period (Bostwick 1988) found for the most part flaked and ground stone scatters with associated rock features. The rock features may have functioned as hearths, roasting pits or platforms, or foundations for brush structures.

In addition to the investigations of the above prehistoric sites, Stein (1988) investigated two historic homesteads. Both were 320-acre units occupied briefly between 1929 and the mid-1930s.

Although not extensive, this information provides at least a limited picture of the region's prehistoric occupation. Known sites represent occupations of limited duration focusing on resource exploitation. Subsurface deposits appear not to be extensive or particularly deep, and feature types seem fairly limited. Complexity is evident in several aspects. However, the ceramic assemblages described for sites near the project area confirm a larger pattern for the area, centering on the presence of sherds associated with both the Hohokam and Patayan ceramic traditions (Stone 1986). Furthermore, analysis of a number of sites recorded during these studies, as well as others located within the region, revealed repeated short-term occupations that had begun as early as the Archaic and persisted into the Historic period.

FIELD METHODS AND EXCAVATION RESULTS

The Flatiron Site (AZ T:5:12, ASM)

Site Description

The Flatiron Site encompassed an extensive area along both sides of Fourmile Wash (Figure 4.1) in T.3N, R.6W, sec. 35, S½NW¼, SW¼. The southern boundary of the site extended from BLM land onto land under private ownership; hence, the exact dimensions of the site are unknown. The portion of the site that was examined during this project measured 875 m north-south by at most 475 m east-west.

The site consisted of a low-density artifact scatter that contained five distinct loci. These loci varied in size and were characterized by artifact densities markedly higher than those of the surrounding area. Numerous rock features visible on the surface as clusters of rock were distributed both within and between these loci. In some areas, these features were clustered in groups of three to six, whereas in other areas they were isolated occurrences.

Recovered artifacts included a variety of ceramics from the Hohokam and Lower Colorado ceramic traditions, as well as locally manufactured varieties. Lithics consisted primarily of cores and flakes of local igneous materials. Ground stone was quite common, and several fragments of shell and argillite jewelry also were recovered.

The site had been substantially disturbed by arroyo cutting and ranching activity. In some areas, particularly the northeast, the site was so eroded that less than half of the original deposits remained. Grazing had increased runoff erosion, and the site had been further damaged by the traffic of herd animals through the area.

Field Methods

The field work at the Flatiron Site was initiated by gridding the entire site into 50 x 50 m units using a transit. These grid squares served as horizontal control units for subsequent activities, the first being a controlled surface collection and mapping of the entire site. Within each unit, researchers recorded the location of all surface features as well as relevant topographic information using tapes or a Brunton compass and tapes. This information was compiled into the site map.

In general, a 100% surface collection was taken from each grid unit. In the vicinity of features, the actual location of tools and diagnostic artifacts was recorded. When artifact clusters were particularly dense, the boundaries of the clusters were recorded during the initial mapping. Once the mapping was completed, clusters were either entirely collected or sampled, depending on their size and density. Most of the eight identified artifact clusters were entirely collected. Locus D, which had an area of 65,000 m², was systematically sampled.

BLM personnel had previously identified relatively dense artifact distributions and subsurface features eroding out of arroyo banks in the northern site area (Stone 1988). Given this information, project investigators presumed that these areas, designated Loci A, B, and C, would be most likely to contain substantial subsurface deposits. Consequently, a series of 15 systematically placed backhoe trenches spaced between 5 m and 30 m apart was excavated at these loci. Only one subsurface feature (Feature 113) was encountered, which later proved to be an occupation surface.

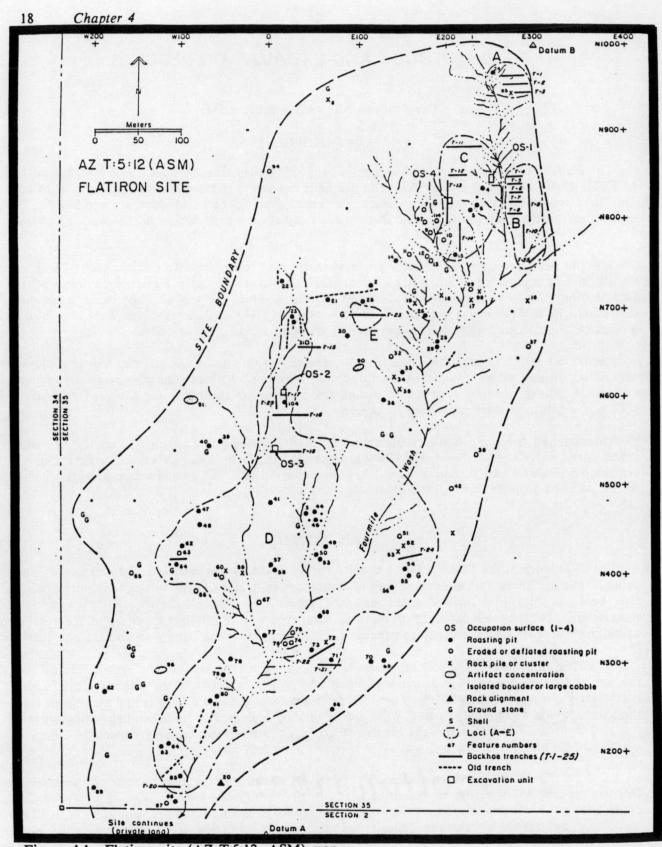

Figure 4.1. Flatiron site (AZ T:5:12, ASM) map.

Once surface collection and mapping were completed, researchers selected additional areas for trenching. A single trench excavated through the approximate center of Locus E failed to produce evidence of subsurface features at this relatively small locus (30 x 35 m). Researchers then excavated 10 trenches within Locus D, 5 of them at the northern extent of the locus where artifact density and diversity were relatively high. Two occupation surfaces (Features 109 and 112) subsequently were identified.

Additional trenches were excavated to determine if subsurface deposits were present near particularly well preserved surface features that had been excavated by hand. Of one trench near Features 64 and 85, two trenches near Features 71, 72, and 73, and two trenches near a series of unexcavated surface features (Features 51 to 56), none yielded evidence of subsurface features or deposits.

Researchers then excavated all subsurface features and a sample of surface features and selected an additional sample of surface features for shovel testing. Controlled excavations used 2 x 2 m grids as the basic unit for horizontal control within the larger grid system. These units, placed to allow the most convenient excavation of features, were designated by the coordinates of their southwest corners.

Controlled excavation of 10 features indicated that the probability of finding subsurface deposits was very low. Researchers then excavated a shovel-width trench through each of 6 additional features to a depth of 30 cm, which confirmed the expectation that subsurface deposits were lacking.

Vertical control was established with reference to Datum B located at N1000/E300. Instrument height at this point was established as the 0 elevation point, resulting in a ground surface elevation of 1.7 m below datum. Subsequent vertical measurements were tied in to this point. Additional data points for excavation were established using an alidade, and all subsequent elevations were recorded as meters below datum.

As a general rule, excavation was by 10 cm arbitrary levels, or by natural or cultural strata when possible. For the most part, excavated material was sifted through quarter-inch mesh screen, and all cultural material was saved. A backhoe removed 30–50 cm of noncultural overburden prior to excavation of Occupation Surfaces 3 and 4. Excavation of half of a 2 x 2 m unit sectioned isolated features, which were then profiled. When warranted, investigators excavated the remaining half and took samples for paleobotanical analysis.

Sampling followed guidelines established in Teague et al. (1982). A photographic record illustrated the range of feature types present, the local environment, and excavation results on 35 mm color slides and black-and-white print film. Scaled plan and profile drawings were made of all excavated features. Researchers used standard SWCA field forms to record information pertaining to the excavation and interpretation of site features. In addition, the supervisory archaeologist recorded project progress and additional observations and interpretations relevant to the excavation in a daily field journal. Field methods employed at the smaller sites followed the basic procedures outlined above.

Feature Descriptions and Excavation Results

During the mapping and surface collection of the site, investigators identified 96 surface features, most commonly rock features, including 75 roasting pits, 12 rock piles, 7 rock clusters, and 15 isolated boulders. Roasting pits consisted of collections of fire-cracked rock that ranged in form from tightly clustered piles to diffuse scatters. Rock piles consisted of non–fire-cracked rocks that occurred as tightly associated piles. Rock clusters consisted of generally loose clusters of rock, either artifactual (ground stone fragments, lithic debris) or nonartifactual cobbles. The isolated boulder category included large boulders that occurred on the surface of the site. Not all of the latter were assigned feature numbers, but examples were photographed and all were mapped. Other surface features included a pot break and one surface artifact concentration.

In addition to the surface features, archaeologists excavated 27 subsurface features (Table 4.1) that included 4 occupation surfaces and associated features as well as roasting pits, a rock alignment, and other thermal features.

Feature 1 (N685/E21.9)

This feature was visible on the surface as a cluster of vesicular basalt and rhyolite cobbles and fire-cracked rock measuring approximately 2 m in diameter. No artifacts were directly associated with the feature. The density of rocks contained within this feature indicated that it represented an intact roasting pit. Excavation of a 1 x 2 m unit through half of the feature found no subsurface deposits; apparently the roasting pit had completely deflated.

Feature 2 (N727.6/E117)

Feature 2 also appeared as a surface cluster of fire-cracked rock 2 m in diameter. The rock included pieces of basalt, andesite, rhyolite, and granitic material. This feature also appeared to represent a subsurface roasting pit. The excavation of a 1 x 2 m unit found fire-cracked rock to a depth of 17 cm. In some areas small pockets of darker soil or charcoal flecks were present, but neither a pit nor subsurface artifacts were present. This feature apparently was the eroded remains of another roasting pit.

Feature 3 (N462.5/E41.5)

Feature 3 was located on the slope of an arroyo. It was visible prior to excavation as a cluster of fire-cracked rock measuring approximately 2 m in diameter. Many of the rocks were partially buried. Excavation revealed a shallow pit measuring 0.8 m in diameter and 15 cm in depth. The pit contained loose, dark gray silt and 18 pieces of fire-cracked rock. No artifacts were recovered from the feature fill. This feature appeared to be the bottom portion of a partially eroded roasting pit.

Feature 20 (N160/W50)

This feature consisted of a concentration of cobbles and boulders distributed over 25 m² (Figure 4.2). The rocks ranged from 10 cm to 30 cm in diameter. Artifacts on the surface included two cores, an obsidian flake, and a mano fragment. This feature was excavated because of the possibility that it represented a temporary structure of some kind. A 0.3 x 5.0 m hand trench to a depth of 0.3 m through the center of the feature revealed that it was a surface manifestation.

Table 4.1. Flatiron Site (AZ T:5:12, ASM) Feature List

Feature Number	Provenience	Description	Feature Number	Provenience	Description
*1	N685 - E21.9	Roasting pit	58	N402 - E05	Roasting pit
*2	N727.6 - E117	Roasting pit	59	N396 - W35	Rock cluster
*3	N462.5 - E41.5	Roasting pit	60	N396 - W52	Rock cluster
4	N835 - E242	Roasting pit	61	N389 - W53	Eroded roasting pit
5	N814 - E233	Roasting pit	62	N427 - W100	Roasting pit
6	N812 - E231	Roasting pit	63	N407 - W104	Probable roasting pit
7	N803 - E167	Probable roasting pit	*64	N407 - W102.9	Roasting pit
8	N710 - E190	Rock cluster	65	N395 - W160	Probable roasting pit
9	N776 - E185	Possible roasting pit	66	N377 - W81	Probable roasting pit
10	N775 - E199	Possible roasting pit	67	N363 - W11	Probable roasting pit
11	N759 - E159	Possible roasting pit	*68	N349 - E57	Roasting pit
12	N753 - E179	Probable roasting pit	69	N301 - E126	Roasting pit
13	N751 - E182	Probable roasting pit	70	N300 - E118	Roasting pit
14	N751 - E145	Roasting pit	*71	N303 - E72	Roasting pit
15	N759 - E212	Roasting pit	72	N319 - E64	Rock cluster
16	N702 - E294	Rock cluster	*73	N308 - E49	Roasting pit
17	N709 - E227	Rock cluster	*74	N319 - E16	Probable roasting pit
18	N710 - E190	Rock cluster	75	N317 - E12	Probable roasting pit
19	N703 - E165	Rock cluster	76	N326 - E19	Probable roasting pit
*20	N160 - W50	Rock alignment	77	N326 - W05	Roasting pit
21	N708 - E34	Roasting pit	78	N300 - W42	Roasting pit
22	N728 - E20	Roasting pit	79	N288 - W50	Roasting pit
23	N686 - E26	Roasting pit	80	N257 - W59	Roasting pit
24	N964 - E28	Roasting pit	81	N253 - W63	Roasting pit
25	N704 - E108	Roasting pit	82	N262 - W189	Roasting pit
26	N687 - E673	Rock cluster	83	N197 - W122	Roasting pit
27	Feature Number Not Assigned		84	N202 - W114	Roasting pit
*28	N691.8 - E174.7	Roasting pit	*85	N169.7 - W76.3	Roasting pit
*29	N691.8 - E174.7	Ash lens	86	N243 - E72	Roasting pit
30	N667 - E89	Roasting pit	87	N131 - W117	Probable roasting pit
31	N658 - E41	Probable roasting pit	88	N135 - W104	Roasting pit
32	N643 - E134	Probable roasting pit	89	N149 - W204	Roasting pit
33	N624 - E150	Roasting pit	90	N628 - E99	Pot break
34	N619 - E142	Rock cluster	91	N590 - W98	Artifact concentration
35	N603 - E144	Rock cluster	92	Feature Number Not Assigned	
36	N595 - E124	Roasting pit	93	N413 - E57	Roasting pit
37	N702 - E289	Probable roasting pit	94	N847 - W04	Probable roasting pit
38	N532 - E235	Probable roasting pit	95	N940 - E278	Rock cluster
39	N548 - W53	Roasting pit	96	N279 - W123	Rock cluster
40	N543 - W69	Roasting pit	*97	N797 - E168	Probable roasting pit
41	N477 - E01	Roasting pit	98	N718 - E236	Rock cluster
42	N494 - E204	Probable roasting pit	99	N716 - E218	Probable roasting pit
43	N444 - E206	Rock cluster	*100	N845.83 - E250.7	Pit in Feature 106.
44	N466 - E51	Roasting pit	101	N695 - E275	Isolated boulder
*45	N840.8 - E248	Pit in Feature 106	102	N430 - W201	Isolated boulder
46	N460 - E53	Roasting pit	*103	N596.3 - E11.8	Pit with metate in Feature 109
47	N465 - W80	Roasting pit	*104	N504 - E7.4	Ash lens
48	N449 - W86	Roasting pit	*105	N536.1 - E0.80	Roasting pit
49	N432 - E70	Roasting pit	*106	N839.83 - E248	Occupation surface
*50	N424.5 - E51.3	Roasting pit	*107	N840.6 - E248.1	Pit within Feature 106
51	N427 - E150	Probable roasting pit	108	Feature Number Not Assigned	
52	N417 - E154	Rock cluster	*109	N597 - E11.2	Occupation surface
53	N416 - E142	Rock cluster	110	Feature Number Not Assigned	
*54	N401 - E152	Roasting pit	*111	N539.6 - E0.1	Fill associated with Feature 105
55	N399 - E161	Roasting pit	*112	N536.1 - E01	Occupation surface
*56	N380 - E139	Roasting pit	*113	N817.8 - E206.4	Burned pit and occupation surface
57	N404 - E04	Roasting pit	114	N788 - E188	Possible roasting pit

*Excavated feature

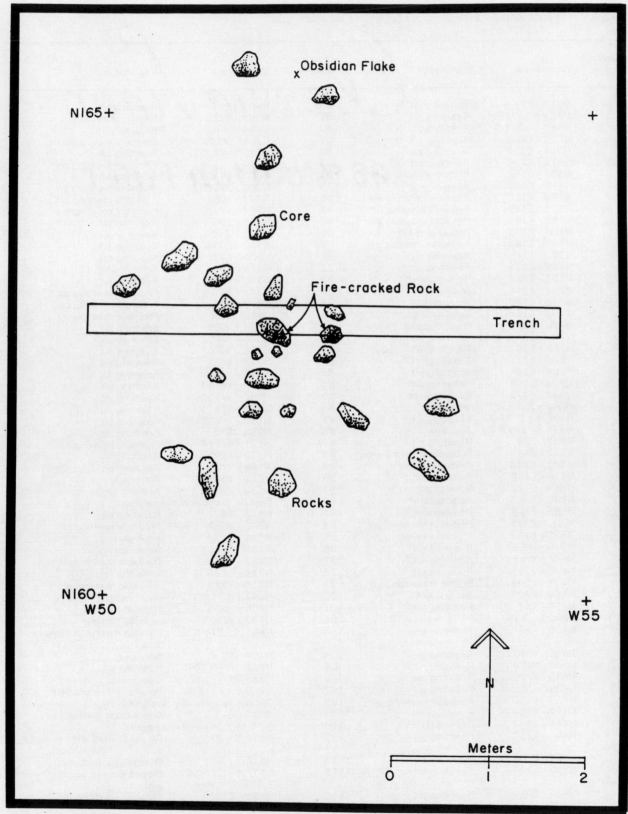

Figure 4.2. Flatiron site (AZ T:5:12, ASM) Feature 20.

Feature 28/29 (N691.8/E174.7)

This feature was identified during the BLM survey (Stone 1988). It appeared as a thin ash lens (Feature 29) visible in the bank of an arroyo cut. Just to the north, a cluster of fire-cracked rock (Feature 28) approximately 0.5 m in diameter rested on the intact arroyo bank.

A profile of the arroyo bank exposed an ash and charcoal lens measuring 1.8 m in length and 20 cm in thickness that had been heavily disturbed by rodent activity. Subsequent excavation of the rock cluster revealed that it was a surface feature. Researchers originally thought that the ash lens might represent the remains of a structure or an occupation surface with an associated roasting pit. However, excavation revealed that what was labeled Feature 28 was in fact fire-cracked rock from the fill of a deflated roasting pit and that Feature 29 represented the ashy pit fill, which had washed downslope to create the ash lens visible in the arroyo bank.

Feature 50 (N424.5/E51.3)

This feature was a deflated roasting pit, visible as a cluster of fire-cracked rock 2 m in diameter confined to the surface. Excavation revealed that very little in the way of subsurface deposits remained. A shallow (12 cm) deposit of slightly ashy soil below the rocks, measuring 60 cm in diameter, contained a few charcoal flecks. No artifacts were associated with this feature, either on the surface or within the subsurface deposits.

Feature 64 (N407/W102.9)

Feature 64 was visible on the surface as a cluster of fire-cracked rock approximately 1 m in diameter. Excavation revealed that the feature was almost exclusively confined to the surface. Immediately below the rocks was a thin (1.0 cm) lens of soil with a diameter of 1.5 m that exhibited a slight ash content and occasional flecks of charcoal. No artifacts were found during excavation. This feature represented a deflated roasting pit.

Feature 71 (N303/E72)

Feature 71 appeared on the surface as a concentration of fire-cracked rock 1.5 m in diameter with an associated dense surface artifact scatter. Excavation revealed that no subsurface deposits were present. Several chunks of charcoal were noted in the excavated soil, but no artifacts were recovered.

Feature 85 (N169.7/W76.3)

Feature 85 was a surface cluster of fire-cracked rock with a diameter of 1.8 m. Excavation determined that no subsurface deposits were present. Subsurface materials included only one sherd and a few charcoal flecks, all of which were encountered within the first 2 cm of the excavation unit.

Feature 104 (N504/E7.4)

This feature consisted of an ash and charcoal deposit of limited extent that was exposed in the walls of Trench 17. The deposit was a depression 25 cm wide and 10 cm deep that was filled with dark gray, ashy silt that contained charcoal chunks. This feature may have been associated with Occupation Surface 2, located 10 m to the north.

Shovel-Tested Features

Because controlled excavation of surface rock features consistently revealed little in the way of subsurface deposits, investigators shovel tested a sample of six additional features, feeling that this approach would efficiently identify any additional features that did, in fact, contain such deposits. Excavation could then be completed in a controlled fashion. However, no subsurface deposits were identified in any of the shovel-tested features (Table 4.2).

Table 4.2. Flatiron Site (AZ T:5:12, ASM) Shovel-Tested Surface Features

Feature Number	Feature Type	Provenience
54	Roasting pit	N401/E152
56	Rock pile	N380/E139
68	Roasting pit	N349/E57
73	Roasting pit	N308/E49
74	Roasting pit	N319/E16
97	Roasting pit	N797/E168

Occupation Surface 1: Features 45, 100, 106, and 107 (N839.83/E248)

Occupation Surface 1 (Figure 4.3) had been heavily eroded by a developing arroyo system. This feature initially was recognized as an ash lens containing bone fragments, visible in a shallow arroyo cut. Only a 4 x 8 m portion of the original feature remained. Eventually five 2 x 2 m units were excavated; although the excavation of additional units would have exposed more of the feature, investigators discontinued the excavation because the partially intact feature would have provided only redundant data.

After excavation, the feature appeared as a tan-brown, compact surface (Feature 106) that contained a number of ash- and charcoal-filled depressions and three pits (Features 45, 100, and 107) containing similar deposits. Feature 45 measured 2.4 m by approximately 0.7 m with a depth of 20 cm. Feature 100 measured 0.9 m in diameter with a depth of approximately 7.0 cm. Feature 107 measured 0.7 x 1.7 m and was 5–10 cm in depth. The fill of these pits was a mottled tan-to-brown silt with darker soil inclusions as well as charcoal chunks and ashy areas. Within the pits and resting on the occupation surface itself were burned fragments of animal bone, occasional fire-cracked rock fragments, locally manufactured plainware sherds, and Sacaton Red-on-buff sherds.

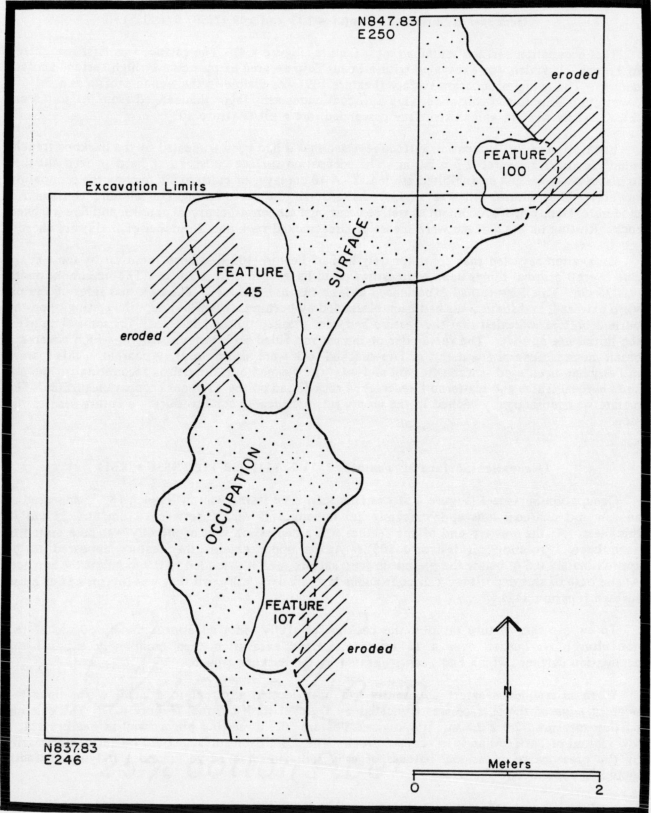

Figure 4.3. Flatiron site (AZ T:5:12, ASM) Occupation Surface 1.

Occupation Surface 2: Features 103 and 109 (N597.9/E11.2)

This occupation surface contained a pit feature (Figure 4.4). The surface was first recognized in Trench 17, which was excavated within Locus D in an area of particularly high surface artifact density. The actual occupation surface (Feature 109) was visible in the trench profile as a 0.1–0.4 cm stratum of oxidized soil underlying a discontinuous ashy layer that ranged from 0.1 to 0.5 cm thick. At its western end this surface descended into a pit (Feature 103).

Excavation of the occupation surface revealed that it had been truncated by the backhoe trench. What remained measured 1.3 x 2.0 m. The occupation surface consisted of hard-packed silt that in places was oxidized or exhibited ash lenses. A 10 cm layer of cultural fill overlay the occupation surface. The cultural fill was slightly darker than the surrounding tan silt and contained a moderately dense artifact content as well as occasional ash lenses, charcoal chunks, and fire-cracked rock. Resting on the surface were pieces of fire-cracked rock and a number of plainware sherds.

Excavation revealed that approximately half of Feature 103 had been removed by the trench. The overall original dimensions were estimated to have been 0.65 x 1.0 m. The maximum depth was 35 cm. This feature had experienced at least two use episodes. The base and sides of the pit were oxidized, and some areas had been blackened by burning. Waterlaid deposits resting upon the burned bottom indicated that the feature had been cleaned out and left open for some time after the initial use episode. The remainder of the pit was filled with tan-brown silt, which covered a basalt metate. Several fragments of fire-cracked rock were also present. Apparently, this feature initially had been used as a roasting pit and was later cleaned out, the debris accounting for the ash and charcoal lenses and scattered fire-cracked rock found on the adjacent occupation surface. The metate was subsequently cached in the empty pit, presumably for use during a future visit to the area.

Occupation Surface 3: Features 1051.7, 111, and 112 (N536.1/E01)

Occupation Surface 3 (Figure 4.5) was first identified in the wall of Trench 18. It appeared as an ash and charcoal lens approximately 2.5 m long and varied between 2 cm and 35 cm in thickness. At the western end of the feature was a depression that eventually was determined to have been a roasting pit (Feature 105). At its upper extent, the feature appeared to be approximately 0.6 m below the present ground surface, and it extended to 0.9 m below the surface. At the base of this deposit lay a discontinuous layer of dark, ashy soil that was interpreted as a use surface (Feature 112).

To expose this feature rapidly, the backhoe carefully removed approximately 50 cm of the noncultural overburden over a 16 m² area. Hand excavation then completely exposed the occupation surface, which had been truncated by the backhoe trench.

When in use, this feature apparently had been located adjacent to a small wash, since the western edge of the surface was truncated by a gravel wash channel (Figure 4.5). The existing portion measured 2.0 x 2.8 m. It contained Feature 105, a roasting pit, as well as Feature 111, a low mound of dark soil and fire-cracked rock. The occupation surface could be defined primarily by the presence of occasional patches of ashy soil, fire-cracked rock, and flat-lying artifacts, including a plainware sherd.

Feature 105 also had been partially removed by the backhoe but was estimated to have originally been about 0.8 m in diameter. The maximum depth of the remaining portion of the feature was

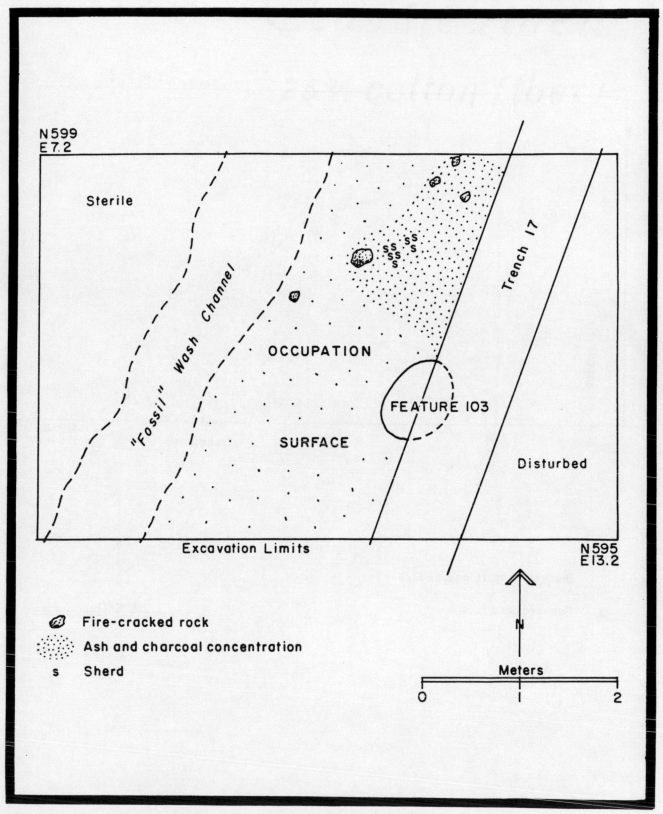

Figure 4.4. Flatiron site (AZ T:5:12, ASM) Occupation Surface 2.

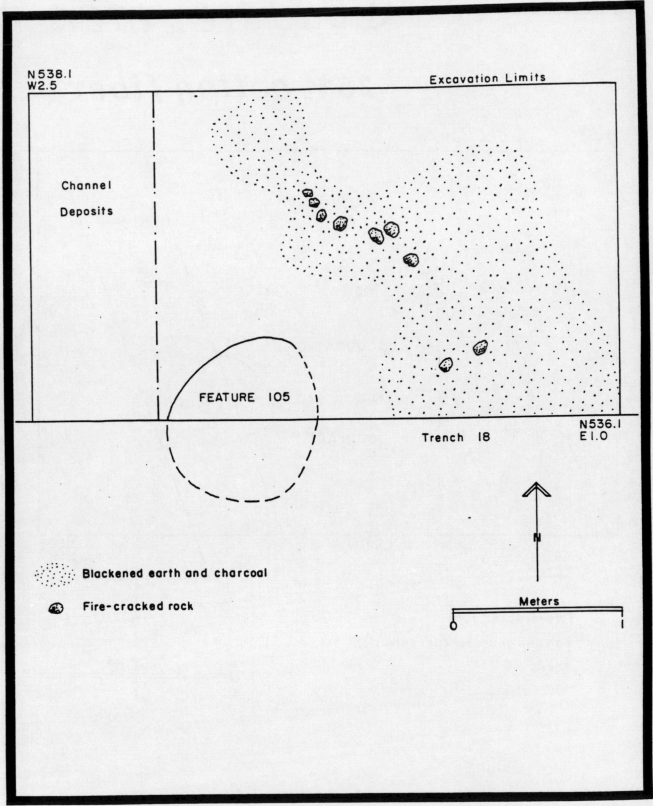

Figure 4.5. Flatiron site (AZ T:5:12, ASM) Occupation Surface 3.

34 cm. Prior to excavation the feature was visible as a semicircular line of oxidized soil, with dark soil and fire-cracked rock inside. Upon excavation the feature was found to be filled with dark gray, ashy soil, charcoal flecks, and abundant fire-cracked rock.

Feature 111 lay adjacent to Feature 105 and consisted of a mound of dark, ashy soil, charcoal chunks, and fire-cracked rock measuring 1.5 x 2.0 m with a thickness of 15–20 cm. A mano and three sherds were recovered from the fill. The sherds included both Patayan and locally made plainware ceramics. The entire feature was lying on the surrounding occupation surface and was evidently fill removed from a use episode of Feature 105.

Immediately west of the roasting pit (Feature 105) was a relict wash channel that apparently had moved to the east after the pit's use, because the eastern edge of the channel gravels had come into contact with the extreme western edge of the pit (Figure 4.5), and subsequent deposition had buried the entire occupation surface under approximately 0.6 m of alluvial fill.

Occupation Surface 4: Feature 113 (N817.8/E206.4)

Feature 113 refers to both a roasting pit and an associated use surface that were exposed in the side wall of Trench 13 (Figure 4.6). Approximately one-third of the feature had been removed by the trench. The pit, irregular in outline, was 14 cm deep and was estimated to have been 0.75 m in diameter. Pit fill consisted of mottled red-brown, gravelly soil containing ash pockets and charcoal fragments. The feature was dug into dense, hard, red-brown, gravelly soil. Resting on this surface were pockets of dark soil, ash, charcoal, and fire-cracked rocks. To the north of the feature was a low (12 cm) mound of darker soil containing fire-cracked rock and ash that measured 0.5 x 0.8 m. The deposit was fill removed from the roasting pit. Waterlaid deposits within the roasting pit and over the surrounding area indicated that the feature had been disturbed by alluvial action soon after its use.

AZ T:5:8(ASM)

Site Description

This site comprised an extremely low density artifact scatter and five features of various kinds (Figure 4.7) distributed over an area that measured 100 x 110 m in T.2N, R.6W, sec. 10, NW¼SE¼. The site lay on the edge of the Fourmile Wash floodplain and extended for approximately 40 m onto a low gravel ridge. Features included four rock features and a lithic reduction locus. During the BLM survey (Stone 1988), nine feature numbers had been assigned, but numbers 5, 6, 7, and 9 either were natural features or were judged to be too far from the site to be included as part of it.

Field Methods

At this site researchers primarily recorded features and collected artifacts, constructing a site map on which the locations of all artifacts were plotted. All artifacts were collected except for ground stone fragments, which generally were just recorded. All features were recorded and photographed. Controlled excavation was conducted at Feature 9, which proved to be a natural occurrence. One other feature was shovel tested.

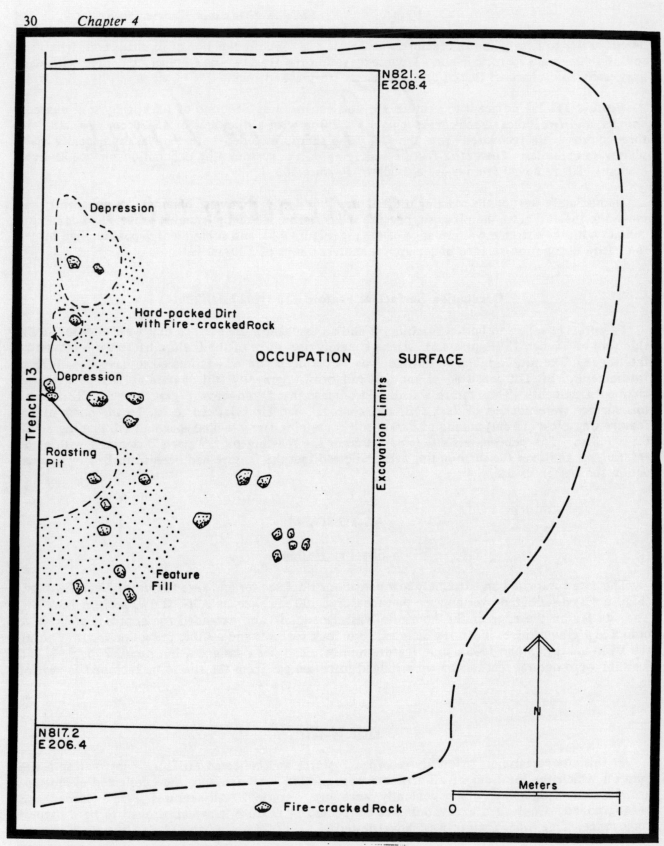

Figure 4.6. Flatiron site (AZ T:5:12, ASM) Occupation Surface 4.

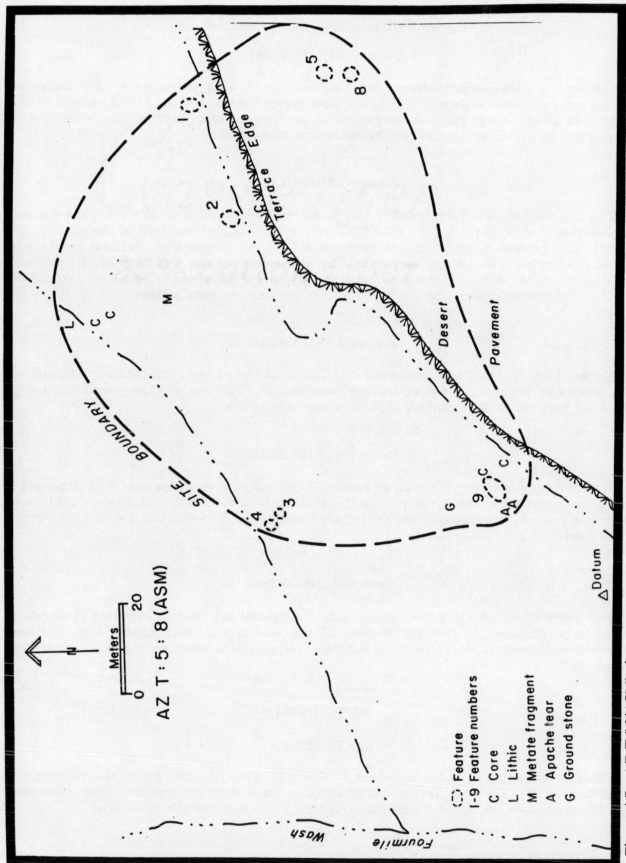

Figure 4.7.　AZ T:5:8(ASM) site map.

Feature Descriptions and Excavation Results

Feature 1 (N116/E208)

Feature 1, a dispersed rock scatter containing fire-cracked rock, measured 5 x 8 m and rested entirely on the ground surface. No artifacts were present on the surface in the vicinity of this feature. In all likelihood, the rock represented a completely deflated roasting pit. Because of its obvious lack of subsurface deposits, this feature was not excavated.

Feature 2 (N108/E182)

This dispersed scatter of fire-cracked rock measured 4.0 m in diameter and contained a cluster of fire-cracked rock measuring 1.0 x 1.73 m. All of the rock was confined to the surface. No artifacts were present. Once again, this feature most likely was a completely deflated or otherwise eroded roasting pit. To test the assumption that the features at this site were strictly surficial, investigators shovel tested Feature 2 and bisected it with a single trench 30 cm deep through the portion judged most likely to be intact. No subsurface deposits were present.

Feature 3 (N100/E118)

Feature 3 was a 2.5 x 3.0 m concentration of fire-cracked rock and local cobbles. All materials were located on the surface, and no artifacts were present. This was another eroded roasting pit where the probability of subsurface deposits was extremely low.

Feature 4 (N101/E116)

Feature 4 lay just to the northwest of Feature 3 and was composed of a cluster of fire-cracked rock and natural cobbles measuring 1 x 2 m. No artifacts were directly associated with this feature, although a ground stone fragment was located 4 m to the north. Like Features 1 through 3, Feature 4 was a deflated or eroded roasting pit.

Feature 8 (N82/E214)

This was a lithic reduction locus at the eastern margin of the site that consisted of numerous fragments of obsidian, all debitage or cores of Apache tears. Several Apache tears had been reduced here to produce flakes for use in cutting or scraping or to serve in the production of more formal tools.

AZ T:5:9(ASM)

Site Description

This site was adjacent to the west bank of Fourmile Wash in T.2N, R.6W, sec. 10, SW¼NE¼, NW¼SE¼, NE¼SW¼, SE¼NW¼. It consisted of an extremely low density artifact scatter covering an area 100 m north-south by 90 m east-west (Figure 4.8). Within the site boundaries

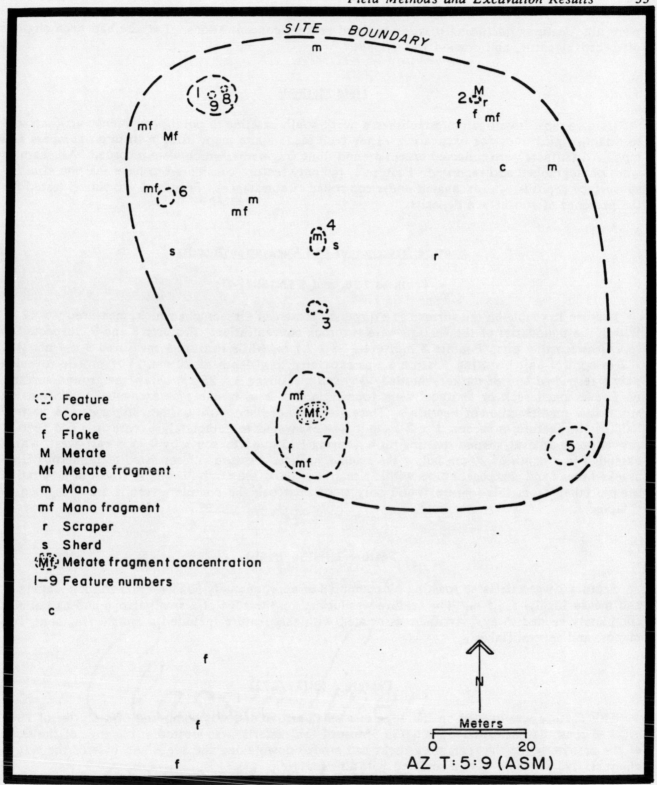

Figure 4.8. AZ T:5:9(ASM) site map.

were nine features, including roasting pits and artifact concentrations. The site had been slightly disturbed by cattle, and erosion was evident.

Field Methods

Using a tape, investigators established a north-south baseline to point provenience artifacts and to establish grid units for excavation. They then made a site map, using a Brunton compass and tape. All artifacts were collected except ground stone fragments, which were recorded. All features were photographed and recorded. Feature 1, the only feature considered to have the potential for subsurface deposits, was excavated under controlled circumstances. Feature 3 was shovel tested for the presence of subsurface deposits.

Feature Descriptions and Excavation Results

Features 1, 8, and 9 (N158/E47)

Feature 1, visible on the surface as a dispersed scatter of fire-cracked rock, measured 9 x 12 m. Within the boundaries of the feature were two rock concentrations, Features 8 and 9, suspected to represent roasting pits. Feature 8 measured 1.8 x 2.1 m, while Feature 9 measured 3 x 4 m. A 1 x 2 m control unit bisecting Feature 8 was excavated to a depth of 20 cm. The profile revealed only a restricted lens of darker, mottled, ashy soil measuring 3 x 25 cm below the ground surface; no fire-cracked rock or artifacts were found. A 1 x 2 m trench was excavated to define the subsurface manifestation of Feature 9. The eastern end of the control unit encompassed the western half of the feature; a second 1 x 2 m unit was excavated to completely expose it. The feature proved to be an oval-shaped roasting pit measuring 1.15 m north-south by 0.75 m east-west, which extended to a depth of 20 cm below the ground surface. Feature fill consisted of numerous fire-cracked rocks and charcoal chunks within a matrix of dark, ashy, sandy soil. Analysis of a flotation sample taken from this feature found only wood charcoal; the complete results are presented in Chapter 7.

Feature 2 (N158/E109)

Feature 2 was a deflated roasting pit composed of approximately 50 fire-cracked rock fragments and measuring 1.1 x 1.5 m. The feature was located on the edge of a small arroyo and had almost completely eroded away. Artifacts associated with this feature included a metate fragment, two manos, and several flakes.

Feature 3 (N111/E72)

This feature was located on the edge of a small arroyo and was composed of a cluster of fire-cracked rock that measured 2.5 x 6.0 m. Most of this material was located at the edge of the slope of the arroyo, while the remaining rocks had eroded down along the edges and base of the arroyo channel. No artifacts were associated with this feature.

Feature 4 (N124/E74)

This 3 x 6 m cluster of fire-cracked rock at the edge of an arroyo had been rapidly eroding away. No artifacts were directly associated with this feature, although one buffware sherd was recovered nearby.

Feature 5 (N68/E124)

Feature 5 was a scatter of dispersed fire-cracked rock and cobbles 15 m in diameter. This feature probably represented the remains of an eroded or deflated roasting pit. Several flaked stone artifacts were recovered from the feature.

Feature 6 (N138/E40)

This was a low-density scatter of fire-cracked rock 3 m in diameter. One basalt mano was associated with the feature, which in all probability represented a deflated roasting pit.

Feature 7 (N80/E66)

Feature 7, located at the southern margin of the site, consisted of a 16 x 22 m scatter of ground and flaked stone artifacts. All materials recovered are listed in the appropriate artifact sections.

AZ T:5:10(ASM)

Site Description

This was a small site, approximately 8 x 10 m in area (Figure 4.9), located in T.2N, R.6W, sec. 10, SE¼NE¼. It consisted of a rock feature and a pot break. The site, on a low ridge 200 m east of Fourmile Wash, was situated on desert pavement, the only vegetation in the area being sparse creosote bush and grasses.

Field Methods

Field procedures at this site consisted of the collection of artifacts and the creation of a site map for the plotting of artifact distributions. The artifacts consisted of sherds from a Lower Colorado Buff Ware jar; the majority of them were found in two clusters, designated Features 2 and 3. Two large sherds representing a substantial portion of the vessel were also present. Feature 1, a rock cluster, was photographed but not redrawn. Because of the disturbed nature of the feature and the low probability of subsurface deposits, no subsurface excavation was conducted.

Feature Descriptions and Excavation Results

Feature 1 (N06/E04), a rock feature measuring 3 x 4 m, was the only feature excavated. It consisted of a diffuse arrangement of local cobbles, primarily rhyolite and basalt, ranging in size from 5 cm to 20 cm in diameter. They were distributed in a single layer, and all appeared to be

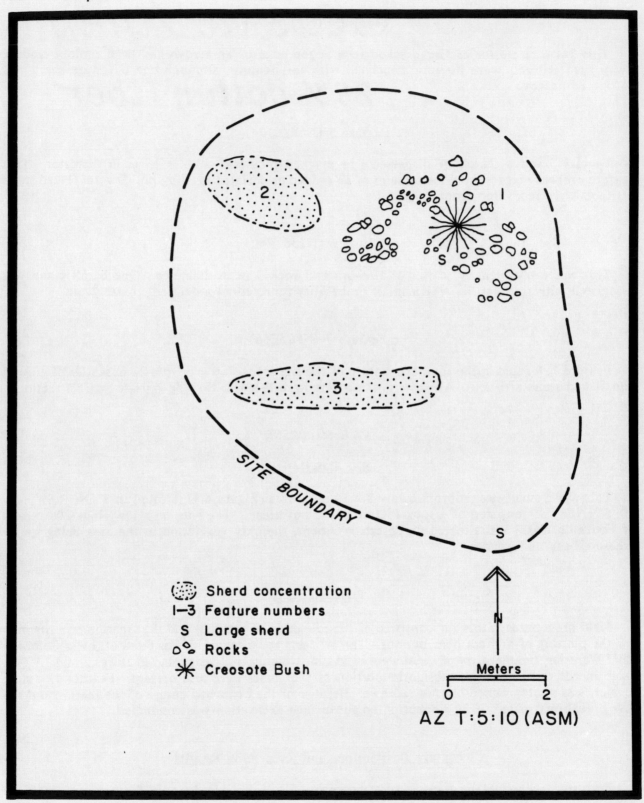

Figure 4.9.   AZ T:5:10(ASM) site map.

resting on the surface. A relatively large creosote bush growing from the center of this feature may have added to its disturbed appearance. Although the exact function of this feature is unknown, given its overall dimensions, it may have been the remains of a temporary structure of some kind, such as a sleeping circle.

AZ T:5:11(ASM)

Site Description

This site was a series of rock features and an associated low-density artifact scatter located in T.3N, R.6W, sec. 35, E½NW¼ (Figure 4.10). Twelve rock piles and one lithic reduction area were distributed over an area measuring 110 m east-west by 140 m north-south on a low ridge adjacent to a small tributary of Fourmile Wash. On the ridge top were a moderately developed desert pavement and a sparse growth of creosote bush.

Field Methods

The site was gridded into 50 x 50 m units that were tied into the grid system established for the Flatiron Site, and all artifacts recovered from a 100% surface collection were point plotted. Feature locations and relevant topographic information, ascertained with a Brunton compass and tapes, were used to produce a site map.

After recording the rock features, investigators noted apparent similarities in form and construction: the features were round to oval in shape, with average minimum dimensions of 0.95 m and average maximum dimensions of 1.2 m, and were constructed of local cobbles taken from the desert pavement. Some features were discrete and obviously cultural. Others, however, were vague and difficult to distinguish from the surrounding desert pavement.

Researchers selected two of the most obvious and well-preserved features for excavation, placing in each a 2 x 2 m unit so that the east-west centerline of the unit would bisect the feature. After features were photographed and drawn in plan, the locations of all associated artifacts were plotted. Next, half of each 2 x 2 m unit was excavated in 10 cm levels to produce a profile. Soil samples for palynological analysis were taken from each feature.

Feature Descriptions and Excavation Results

Feature 1 (N1172/E295.3)

Feature 1, near the southern site boundary, consisted of two adjacent rock features. Feature 1a was a cluster of local cobbles of andesite, rhyolite, and granite that measured 1.0 x 1.5 m and was 15 cm in height. The rocks averaged 10–15 cm in maximum dimension. No fire-cracked rock was observed. Associated with this feature were several plainware sherds, flakes, and a core/scraper. Feature 1b was located 3 m north of Feature 1a and was similar in form and construction, measuring 1 x 2 m. Since Feature 1a was one of the most distinct features at the site, resesarchers selected it for further investigation. Excavation proved that this was strictly a surface feature created by collecting and piling together a group of cobbles that were somewhat larger than

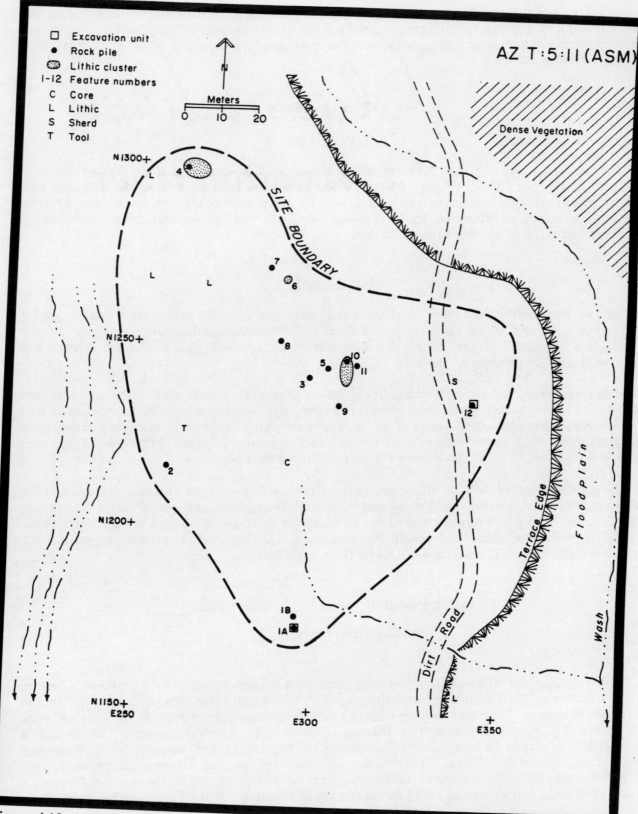

Figure 4.10.   AZ T:5:11(ASM) site map.

those naturally occurring in the area (Figure 4.11). The soil underlying the feature was a loose, tan, silty sand with a high gravel content (approximately 60%).

Excavation immediately following a night and early morning of persistent, moderate rain revealed that moisture had penetrated to a slightly greater depth below the rocks of the feature than into the surrounding surface. This observation holds interesting implications for the suggestion that these features were related to agriculture.

Feature 2 (N1216/E259)

This feature consisted of a poorly defined cluster of local basalt and rhyolite cobbles measuring 1.2 x 1.4 m. No artifacts were found in association with this feature, and none of the cobbles appeared to have been fire cracked.

Feature 3 (N1241/E297)

Feature 3, a dispersed rock scatter measuring 1.03 x 1.45 m, appeared to be strictly surficial and may have represented a disturbed rock ring or rock cluster. It was composed of approximately 30 local cobbles, and several fragments of fire-cracked rock were also noted. No artifacts were found in association with this feature.

Feature 4 (N1298/E264)

This low-density scatter of lithic artifacts measured 5.0 x 7.0 m. The scatter was associated with a dispersed distribution of local cobbles, possibly the remains of a rock ring or cluster, which appeared to be confined to the surface and measured 0.5 x 0.7 m. No fire-cracked rock was noted.

Feature 5 (N1239/E302)

Feature 5 was a 1.1 x 0.8 m dispersed surface rock feature similar to Features 3 and 4 that may have been the remains of a rock cluster or ring. No artifacts or fire-cracked rock were observed.

Feature 6 (N1268/E 290)

This feature was a light scatter of lithics measuring 1.3 m in diameter.

Feature 7 (N1271/E285)

This cluster of local cobbles (rhyolite, basalt, and quartzite) measuring 1.2 x 1.3 m was relatively well defined. It was visible as a group of cobbles that appeared to have been gathered from the immediate vicinity into a low pile. No fire-cracked rock was found, but several flakes were noted.

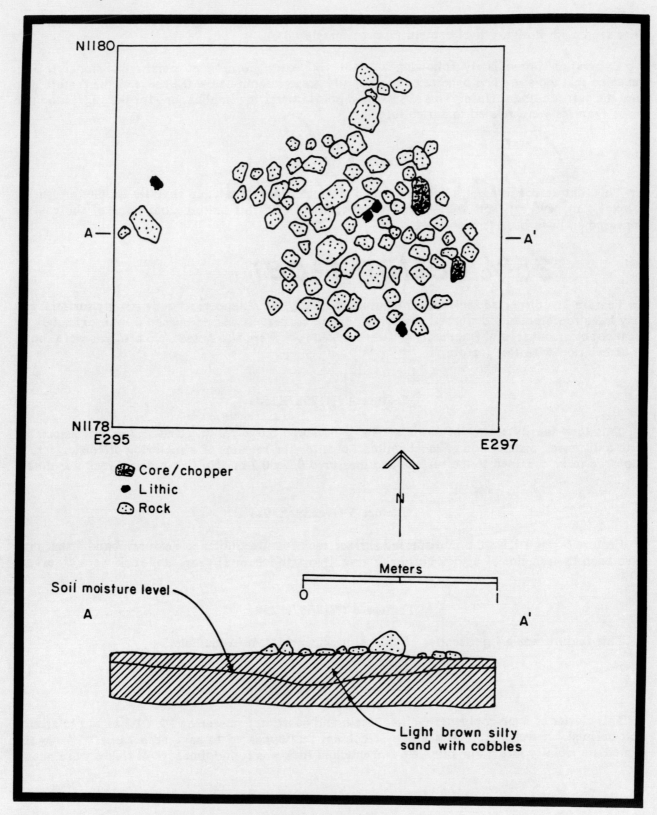

N1180

A ———

A'———

N1178
E295   E297

Core/chopper
Lithic
Rock

N

Meters
0   1

Soil moisture level

A   A'

Light brown silty
sand with cobbles

Figure 4.11.   AZ T:5:11(ASM) Feature 1 plan and profile.

Feature 8 (N1251/E289)

Feature 8 was a concentration of cobbles and possibly fire-cracked rock measuring 1.4 x 1.5 m. Several flakes were associated with this feature.

Feature 9 (N1244/E289)

Measuring 1.5 x 1.9 m, this feature was an oval-shaped concentration of 150 to 175 cobbles including rhyolite, basalt, and quartzite. It appeared to be confined to the surface. Several fragments of fire-cracked rock and a number of lithics were associated with this feature.

Feature 10 (N1246/E307)

Feature 10 was a 4 x 8 m scatter of lithic artifacts. Also present was a cluster of cobbles measuring 0.4 x 0.6 m. No fire-cracked rock was noted, and the feature appeared to be confined to the surface.

Feature 11 (N1245/E309)

This surficial rock cluster measured 0.6 x 1.1 m. It was somewhat dispersed and may have represented the remains of a rock ring. No fire-cracked rock was present.

Feature 12 (N1235/E341)

This feature was located near the eastern boundary of the site and was visible as a discrete cluster of cobbles measuring 0.75 x 1.0 m (Figure 4.12). The cobbles were primarily basalt, although granite cobbles were present as well.

Excavation procedures were the same for this feature as for Feature 1 and revealed that this was also strictly a surface feature, composed of a layer of cobbles placed together on the desert pavement. Unlike Feature 1, the soil was not damp to any greater degree beneath this feature than adjacent to it. Associated with the feature were rhyolite and chalcedony flakes and cores.

AZ T:5:14(ASM)

Site Description

This site was located on the boundary of the project area in T.2N, R.6W, sec. 10, NW¼NE¼ and extended onto private property for some unknown distance. The investigated portion of the site measured 100 m north-south by 120 m east-west (Figure 4.13). The site consisted of a very low density artifact scatter and four rock features. Located adjacent to a modern tank and well, the site had in some areas experienced heavy surface disturbance from cattle congregating near this facility. A dirt road passing through the western portion of the site had also disturbed the surface.

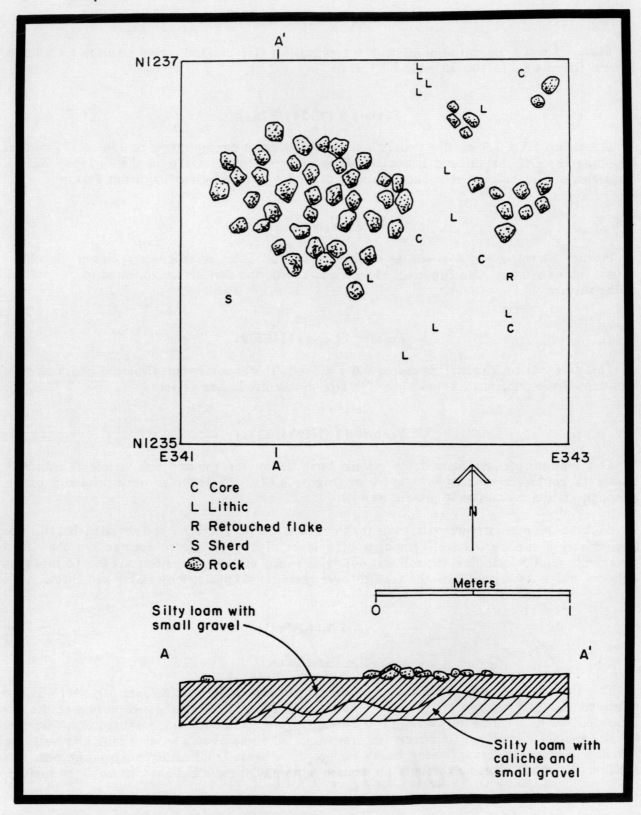

Figure 4.12.   AZ T:5:11(ASM) Feature 12 plan and profile.

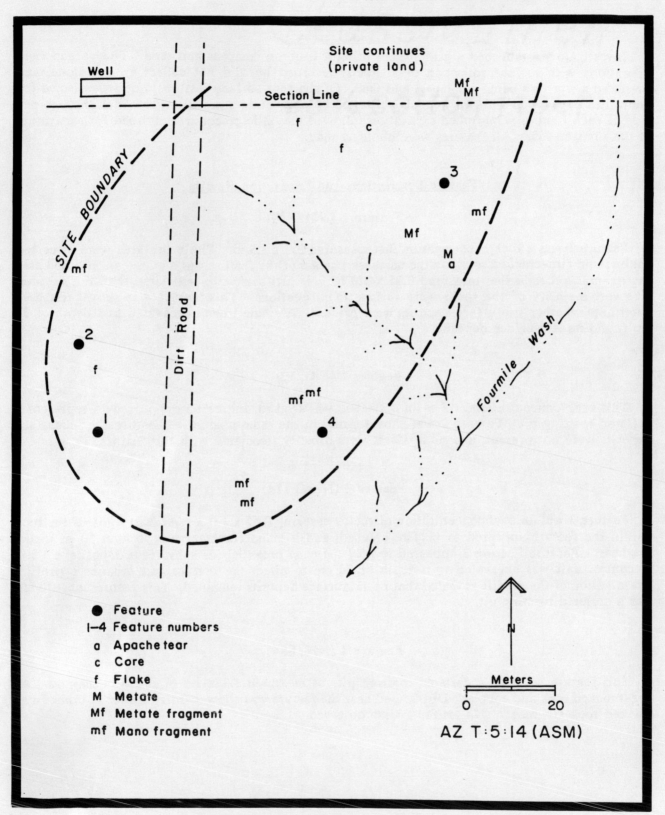

Figure 4.13. AZ T:5:14(ASM) site map.

Field Methods

Investigators established a grid system using a Brunton compass and tape. They began field operations with surface collection of artifacts, recorded but did not collect ground stone, and prepared a site map using a compass and tape. Of the four surface features, one was selected for controlled excavation and two were shovel tested by excavating a shovel-wide trench through one side of each feature. Controlled excavation followed the basic procedures outlined for excavation at the Flatiron Site. All features were photographed.

Feature Descriptions and Excavation Results

Feature 1 (N21/E33)

Feature 1 was a rock concentration that measured 2.7 x 3.5 m. Within this area were dispersed cobbles and fire-cracked rock. In the northern portion of the feature was a more concentrated area of fire-cracked rock that measured 0.75 x 1.0 m. No artifacts were associated with this feature. The vast majority of the rocks were surface manifestations. This feature was shovel tested to determine whether subsurface deposits were present. A single trench excavated to a depth of 30 cm found no subsurface deposits.

Feature 2 (N41/E30)

This rock concentration, 1.5 m in diameter, was oval in outline and appeared to represent a deflated roasting pit. Feature 2 was shovel tested in the same manner as Feature 1. Subsurface deposits were not present, and no artifacts were directly associated with this feature.

Feature 3 (N78/E114)

Feature 3 was an oval concentration of rock measuring 0.65 x 1.0 m. At least some of the rock within the feature appeared to be fire cracked, and a mano fragment was located 10 m to the southeast. Because Feature 3 appeared to hold the most potential for subsurface deposits, a 1 x 2 m control unit was excavated to a depth of 20 cm to bisect the feature and produce a profile. Examination of the profile revealed that no subsurface deposits remained. This feature most likely was a deflated roasting pit.

Feature 4 (N20/E84)

This feature was also a deflated roasting pit. It measured 1.3 x 1.5 m and was composed of fire-cracked rock and cobbles. Distributed near the feature was a low-density scatter of other fire-cracked rock fragments. No artifacts were observed.

AZ T:5:16(ASM)

Site Description

Site AZ T:5:16(ASM) was located in T.2N, R.6W, sec. 10, SE¼NE¼, in an interdrainage area over 600 m east of Fourmile Wash. Lying between an ephemeral rill and an area of desert pavement, the site contained three clusters of apparently fire-cracked rock (Figure 4.14) and measured 8 x 14 m overall. Although the BLM survey crew recorded three cores at the site, these could not be relocated during data recovery. No other artifacts were present.

Field Methods

Using a Brunton compass and tape, investigators prepared a site map that located site features in relation to local topography. They then inspected the area for artifacts but found none. Due to the dispersed nature of the features and the lack of artifacts, controlled excavation was deemed unwarranted. The features were photographed, then shovel tested by excavation of a shovel-wide trench 30 cm deep through one side of each feature.

Feature Descriptions and Excavation Results

Feature 1

Feature 1 consisted of a 1.5 x 2.25 m scatter of fire-cracked rock and cobbles. In an area measuring 0.5 x 0.8 m in the southwestern portion of the feature the distribution of rock was considerably more dense. Rock size ranged from 4 cm to 10 cm in diameter. A shovel trench excavated through the southern portion of the feature revealed no associated subsurface deposits. The fire-cracked rock extended only 3 cm to 5 cm below the present ground surface.

Feature 2

Feature 2 measured 1.75 x 2.0 m and consisted of an area of dispersed fire-cracked rock. Rock size ranged from 8 cm to 20 cm, and material types included basalt, granite, and rhyolite. A 0.6 x 0.7 m area of denser rocks was located in the center of the larger scatter. Excavation revealed no subsurface deposits.

Feature 3

The dispersed scatter of rock composing Feature 3 measured 3.0 x 1.75 m and consisted of approximately 40 rocks ranging in size from 4 cm to 10 cm in diameter. Material types included basalt, rhyolite, and granite. Excavation of an east-west trench through the middle of the feature showed no subsurface deposits.

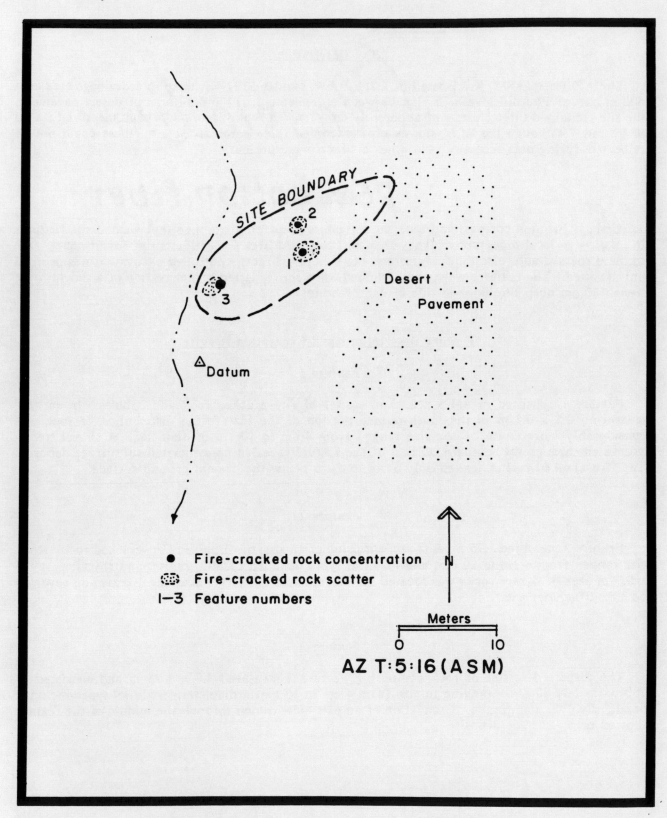

Figure 4.14.   AZ T:5:16(ASM) site map.

AZ T:5:17(ASM)

Site Description

This site, located in T.3N, R.6W, sec. 34, NE¼NE¼, measured 65 m east-west by 75 m north-south. It consisted of four features and a low-density artifact scatter (Figure 4.15). Three of the features were evident on the surface as concentrations of rock and artifacts. The fourth feature consisted of a cluster of rocks 8.0 m in diameter. The site was adjacent to a small wash forming the west fork of Fourmile Wash and supporting a relatively dense desert riparian vegetation association. The surrounding level alluvial plain is otherwise devoid of vegetation save for a few stunted creosotes and various annuals and grasses.

Field Methods

Investigators prepared a site map using a compass and tapes, then collected all artifacts visible on the surface and either point-plotted them or collected them by features. All features were then photographed and recorded. Features 2 and 5 were selected for controlled excavation.

Feature Descriptions and Excavation Results

Feature 1 (N56/E57)

This dispersed cluster of artifacts and rhyolite and basalt cobbles measured 7 x 10 m. None of the rocks had been thermally altered. The artifacts included sherds, lithics, and a hammerstone. All of the rocks associated with this feature rested on the ground surface.

Feature 2 (N72/E27)

Feature 2 was a rock cluster and associated artifact scatter that measured 10 x 19 m overall. The rock cluster measured 10 m in diameter and consisted of a dispersed group of rhyolite and basalt cobbles averaging 3–5 cm in diameter. These cobbles had not been fire cracked. The area around the cobbles was also markedly higher in gravel content than was the general site surface. Artifacts present included ceramics, lithics, and ground stone.

Investigators excavated a 2 x 2 m unit within Feature 2 to determine whether subsurface features or deposits were present. They placed this unit in the eastern half of the feature within the area that exhibited a higher gravel content because of the possibility that the gravel and rocks were the remains of a prehistoric structure. Excavation to a depth of 20 cm showed no subsurface features. The only artifacts present were several sherds in the initial 5 cm of the level.

Features 3 (N60/E12) and 5 (N85/E18)

Feature 3 was an artifact scatter measuring 15 x 40 m that was composed of ceramics, a variety of flaked and ground stone, cobbles, and rock fragments. At the northern end of the feature was a low-density cluster of cobbles and rock fragments; artifact density here was somewhat higher than elsewhere within the feature. Several fragments of animal bone and ashy soil noted on the surface within this area were designated Feature 5 (Figure 4.16).

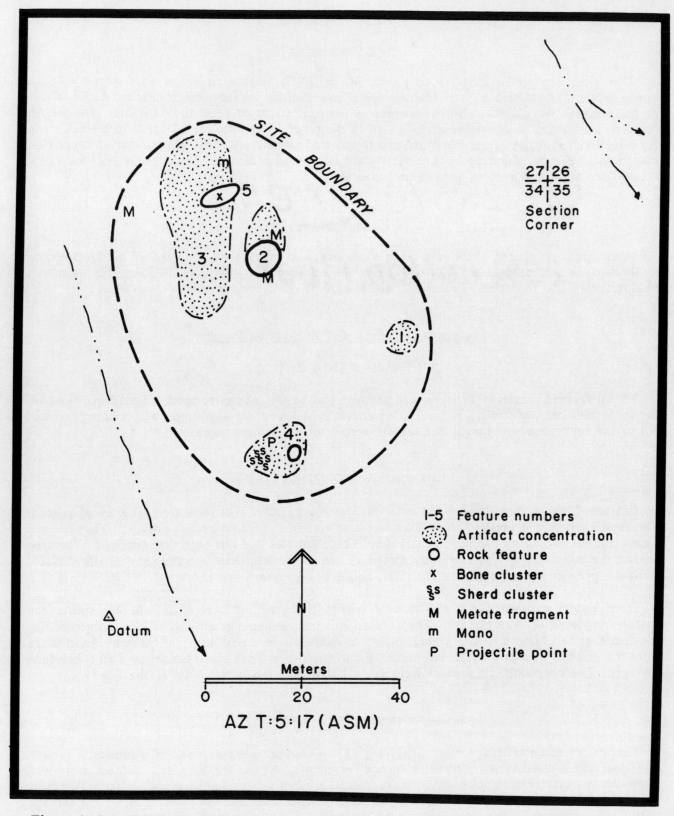

Figure 4.15. AZ T:5:17(ASM) site map.

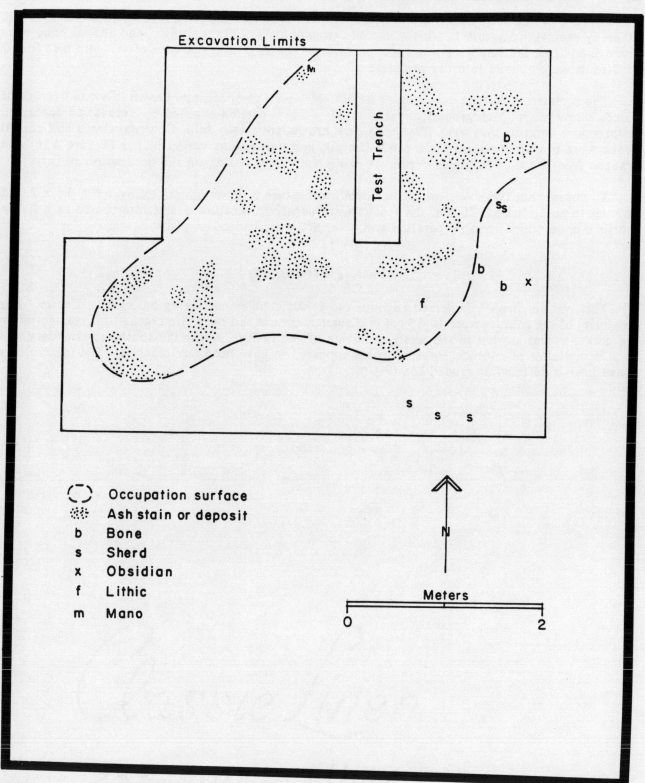

Figure 4.16. AZ T:5:17(ASM) Feature 5 plan and profile.

A 2 x 2 m unit encompassing Feature 5 was trowelled and shovel scraped to a depth of 4 cm, thereby removing Stratum 1, a loose, tan-brown silty loam. Sherds, lithics, and animal bone were recovered from Stratum 1. An occupation surface was located at the base of this stratum; four 2 x 2 units were opened in order to define it.

The occupation surface consisted of a relatively level, compact, tan-brown layer an average of 5 cm below the modern ground surface. A 3.0 x 5.5 m portion exposed by excavation contained depressions and pits that were filled with dark brown, silty, ashy soil. Charcoal flecks and animal bone were prevalent within these pits. The pits and depressions varied in size (Figure 4.16) and ranged from 2 cm to 20 cm in depth. A mano was found resting on the occupation surface.

To ensure that there was no further depth to Feature 5, investigators excavated a 0.5 x 2.0 m trench to an additional 20 cm; the results were negative. Feature 5 was interpreted as a living surface upon which food preparation and other activities had taken place.

Feature 4 (N33/E27)

This was an area of dispersed rhyolite and basalt cobbles measuring 8.0 m in diameter. The majority of the cobbles were 10–15 cm in diameter; several had been fire cracked. A concentration of ceramics was located in the western portion of the feature. Near the southeast boundary was a 0.75 m cluster of cobbles, some of which appeared to have been fire cracked. The feature may have been a deflated or eroded roasting pit.

5

ARTIFACT ANALYSES

CERAMICS

Arthur W. Vokes

Five of the Fourmile Wash sites produced ceramic materials, with a total of 2,397 sherds recovered (Table 5.1). The bulk of the assemblage (61%) was composed of plainware sherds, most of which appeared to have been of local origin, although two Hohokam Plain Ware types, Wingfield Plain and Gila Plain, Gila Variety, also were represented. The assemblage contained both Hohokam Buff Ware and Lower Colorado Buff Ware, as well as a buffware that is probably of local origin. A minor amount of redware was present in the assemblage, and once again locally manufactured material as well as Hohokam and Lower Colorado types were represented. Verde Black-on-gray, a Northern Arizona whiteware of undetermined type, and sherds of Tizon Brown Ware representing a single vessel also were recovered.

Methods

The western desert regions of Arizona have been largely overlooked by archaeologists. In general, controlled excavations and systematic surveys have been few and of limited scope. As a result, the nature of the ceramic assemblages and their relationship to those of the surrounding, more thoroughly investigated regions, is poorly understood. Therefore, it was necessary to approach the material collected during the Fourmile Wash investigations as a previously undefined assemblage.

The initial step in the analysis was to become familiar with the gross characteristics of the assemblage by reviewing a sample of the collections. Although types representing the principal ceramic traditions of southern Arizona were present, the bulk of the material appeared to represent previously undefined types. This material often exhibited attributes similar to those of known types, suggesting that the material may have simply represented regional or even local variation within previously defined ceramic traditions. The samples were not large enough to demonstrate affinity. In addition, most of the material was derived from the surface of the sites, thereby precluding observations of temporal associations other than those achievable on the general site level.

All of the sherds collected were examined with a 10X handlens and then sorted into previously defined types and several newly defined types. During this process, researchers recorded the characteristics of the ceramics and selected a sample that provided the basis for the type descriptions below. Emphasis was placed on identifying the distinctive characteristics of the material. Upon completion of the analysis, researchers reviewed the samples and notes regarding the similarities of the field types and combined several. In those cases where the sample was very small, principally in the case of buffwares, the specimens were placed in an unidentified category under the appropriate general class of material.

Plainwares

The plainware assemblage was dominated by brownware sherds, which appeared to have been locally produced. Five local types were recognized and defined. The Hohokam types, Wingfield Plain and Gila Plain, Gila Variety, were represented by a much smaller number of sherds. The

Table 5.1. Ceramics from the Fourmile Wash Project

Ceramic Types	Site Numbers (AZ T:5: , ASM)					Total
	9	10	11	12	17	
Hohokam Tradition						
Sacaton Red-on-buff				31		31
Santa Cruz Red-on-buff				1		1
Sacaton/Santa Cruz Red-on-buff				1		1
Unidentified Red-on-buff				24		24
Unidentified buffware				106	1	107
Sacaton Red				6		6
Wingfield Plain			1	25	1	27
Gila Plain, Gila Variety				45		45
Patayan Tradition						
Palomas Red-on-buff				1		1
Type 1 Red-on-buff				2		2
Type 2 Red-on-buff				6		6
Type 3 Red-on-buff				4		4
Type 1 buffware	2			32	103	137
Type 2 buffware				73	67	140
Type 3 buffware			8	205	8	221
Unidentified buffware				13		13
Type 1 redware				6		6
Type 2 redware				30	9	39
Unidentified redware				2		2
Local Tradition Plainware						
Type A			6	1163	23	1192
Type B				114		114
Type C			2	13	3	18
Type D				54		54
Type E			7			7
Other Types						
Verde Black-on-gray				28		28
Unidentified northern Arizona whiteware				1		1
Aquarius Brown		169				169
Unidentifiable Sherds					1	1
Total	2	169	24	1986	216	2397

majority of the sherds representing these Hohokam types were recovered from one site, and none was recovered from excavated contexts. The low frequency of these well-known types may reflect exchange or other forms of contact with the Hohokam communities to the east and south of the project area. Alternatively, they may indicate occasional use of the Fourmile Wash area by Hohokam groups. The local material was divided into the following types on the basis of tempering material, paste characteristics, and surface treatment.

Type A Local Plainware

Construction

Paddle and anvil construction was indicated by anvil impressions on the interiors of a number of jar sherds. Bowl sherds tend not to exhibit these features as clearly, due to the finishing of the vessel surfaces. Wall thickness ranged from approximately 3 mm to 10 mm, with considerable variation often present on a single vessel. Some bowls thickened markedly near the rim.

Core

Core color ranged from medium or reddish brown to light gray. Considerable color variation was often present in the cross section of individual sherds. The texture of the paste, though variable, was generally quite coarse.

Temper

Temper ranged from rounded particles of quartz sand to subangular particles of quartz and feldspar. The size of the particles varied considerably, with a general positive correlation between angularity and particle size. There was a low incidence of rock particles in the specimens, generally micaceous schist, gneiss, and an unidentified dark material. These particles tended to be quite angular and may have represented the addition of crushed rock to the paste. In a number of examples, flecks of mica were relatively common throughout the paste. The tempering material was abundant, ranging from one-third to over one-half the volume of the sherds.

Fracture

This type had a relatively crumbly fracture that tended to leave an uneven face. The amount and size of the temper particles influenced the degree to which the face appeared uneven.

Surface

Surface color was variable, with the majority of sherds ranging from orange-red to brownish beige. Silver- and gold-colored mica flecks were often present on the surface. Fire clouding was present but did not appear to be common or patterned. The exposed surfaces had been finished by wiping or polishing. Some specimens appeared to have been finished by simply wiping the surface with a cloth or a similar material. Other examples had been given a cursory polishing, and still others had been quite carefully and thoroughly polished. There were no instances where the polishing resulted in a highly polished surface with a floated slip. As a result of the variability of finish, the texture of the surface also varied, ranging from a medium to a relatively coarse surface.

Forms

Bowl and jar forms were represented in the sample. The bowls had direct rims, which often had been squared off by flattening at the top, producing a noticeable thickening of the vessel wall in the area contiguous to the rim. Vessel sizes were difficult to estimate, as the majority of the sherds were quite small. Measurable bowl rims indicated diameters of approximately 20 cm.

Jars were quite variable in size, ranging from medium-sized cooking or storage vessels to large ollas. A number of sherds were recovered that exhibited a modified shoulder form, having an internal angle of approximately 120–130°. The jar necks were quite short, averaging approximately 2.5 cm in height, and were turned directly upward. As with the bowls, many of the jar rim sherds had been given a squared profile by flattening the rim.

Comment

This was by far the most common type recovered from the excavations.

Type B Local Plainware

Construction

Manufacture probably had been by paddle and anvil, although few sherds retained any direct evidence, as the surfaces had been too well finished.

Core

Core color ranged from dark gray to orange-red. Often there was considerable gradation across the profile of the sherds. This material had been fired at relatively high temperatures, which resulted in some of the paste taking on a somewhat vitrified appearance. The paste texture was fine to medium. In some specimens, narrow voids or parting planes paralleling the surfaces were observed. These may have been produced when the paste had been compacted during the construction of the vessel.

Temper

Tempering material was dominated by subangular particles of quartz, both clear and white, and feldspar. Calcium carbonate occasionally was present. Sherd temper also was present in low frequency in a number of specimens. Overall, the temper was moderately abundant, accounting for one-third to one-half of the total volume of the sherds. Very fine particles of mica were found in the paste of a number of sherds. The fineness of the material, however, suggested that it had been derived from the clay source and had not been added as temper material.

Fracture

The break generally was sharp and clean with little crumbling. This appeared to be due to the hardness of the paste caused by high firing temperatures.

Surface

Exterior surfaces generally were well polished and very even, but often pitted. This pitting appeared to be primarily the result of gas vesicles opening to the surface. Some pits had been produced by surface exfoliation over temper particles. Surface texture tended to be very fine, although a few sherds exhibited a moderately coarse surface. Surface color ranged from tan-beige to brick red, the latter appearing to coincide with the high-fired sherds. Fire clouding was relatively common on vessel exteriors, but no specimens were large enough to allow identification of patterned fire clouds.

Forms

Both bowls and jars were present in the sample, with the former somewhat more common. Rim sherds indicated that vessel shapes were limited to medium-sized jars and bowls with direct rims. Since no jar rims were identified, there was no way to identify the form of these vessels.

Type C Local Plainware

Core

Construction of the vessels had been by paddle and anvil, identified by the anvil marks present on the interior surface of some jar sherds. Core color ranged from reddish brown to dark brown. The vessels represented appeared to have been fired at a relatively low temperature. The texture of the clay was quite coarse.

Temper

Temper was dominated by rounded, clear quartz sand, although rare particles of opaque, white quartz were observed. A dark material, with a crystalline structure similar to garnet, was the second most common tempering component, although it was also relatively rare in comparison to the clear quartz. In general, the tempering material was fine, with occasional particles visible to the unaided eye. Temper accounted for approximately one-third of the volume.

Fracture

Due to the relatively soft nature and coarse texture of the material, the specimens tended to crumble when broken.

Surface

Surface color paralleled core color, ranging from reddish brown to dark brown. The surfaces had ample quantities of fine flecks of gold mica. The mica was definitely part of the general paste; however, it was so fine that it was not easily observed in the cross section and did not constitute a significant part of the volume. Surfaces had been smoothed but not generally polished, resulting in a somewhat rough feel.

Forms

All of the sherds for which form could be determined appeared to be from jars. No rim sherds were recovered.

Type D Local Plainware

Construction

Construction probably had been by paddle and anvil, although no clear evidence for construction technique was observed. Subtle indentations were present on the interior surface of some sherds.

Core

Paste color varied from dark gray to light grayish beige. The sherds appeared to have been fired at high temperatures, as the paste was quite hard and resistant to erosion. Texture was somewhat variable, ranging from very fine (nearly invisible) to medium. The paste often had a layered appearance, with narrow gaps paralleling the surfaces. In some instances these voids were filled with a soft white precipitate, possibly calcium carbonate. The specimens with the more granular texture appeared to contain more silt in the clay mixture.

Temper

Temper was predominately rolled sand with some angular particles. The sand was primarily white quartz with some clear grains present. A thin scatter of dark, opaque material was visible throughout the paste. The tempering material tended to be quite small and represented less than one-quarter of the overall volume.

Fracture

The break of the sherds was quite sharp and clean.

Surface

Surface color ranged from medium to reddish brown. Exterior surfaces were generally well polished. In some cases, polishing had created a float or false slip.

Forms

Both jars and bowls were represented. The bowls had direct rims. No examples of jar rims or necks were observed. None of the vessels appeared to be very large.

Type E Local Plainware

This type was recovered only from AZ T:5:11(ASM) and in limited quantity. It is included here as a separate type due to its unusual character and its presence in collections from other projects.

The type was represented by seven jar sherds recovered from a discrete concentration, probably the remains of a single vessel.

This type is characterized by large temper particles of crushed granitic rock. A similar type was reported by Huckell (1979:48–50) as Temper Group 2 in the assemblage recovered from the Lago Seco Site on Luke Air Force Base. This was a minor type at Lago Seco but accounted for a greater portion of the assemblage than is the case with the Fourmile Wash material. Little can be said of the Fourmile Wash specimens other than that they represented a single vessel with a smoothed exterior surface that originally may have been polished. The surfaces of the specimens were heavily eroded in some cases. Paste and surface color was light red.

Buffwares

The buffwares recovered appeared to have been derived from three sources: the Hohokam, groups residing along the lower Gila and Colorado rivers, and local production. The first two traditions have been reported on elsewhere and therefore do not warrant full type descriptions. The local material has not been so treated prior to this study. Three principal types existed in the sample; all seemed to have been heavily influenced by the Patayan traditions and might be viewed as local variants of those traditions. Technologically, the main influence appeared to have been from the south, where populations along the lower Gila River produced Palomas Buff, a type characterized by rolled sand temper (Schroeder 1958; Waters 1982:293), the principal component of the locally produced material. The following type descriptions pertain to more than 97% of the non-Hohokam material. The remaining sherds did not fall within the established type descriptions and were too few in number to develop adequate descriptions.

Type 1 Buffware

Core

Paste color was generally reddish beige. Some areas associated with fireclouds had a light gray color. Texture was quite coarse, with the granular structure of the paste readily visible with a hand lens.

Temper

Temper was a distinguishing feature of this type. It was a mixture of sherd particles and rolled quartz sand, approximately equal in volume within the cross sections. The sherd temper appeared as reddish or brownish-red particles, some of which were large enough to contain particles of tempering material of their own. Occasional inclusions of calcium carbonate were present. Temper was abundant, occupying up to 50% of the sherd volume.

Fracture

The sherds fractured cleanly, with relatively little crumbling.

Surface

Exterior surfaces exhibited a buff-colored wash or slip and were unpolished, with a medium texture. Faint wiping striae were observed on some of the sherds.

Forms

Jars were the dominant form represented in the sample. Only one jar rim sherd was recovered. This single sherd represented a vessel with a wide aperture (approximately 19 cm in diameter). The neck and rim were short and upturned in section. Several body sherds showed evidence of a low, modified shoulder.

Decoration

Red paint was noted on one sherd, but there was not enough to determine the design.

Type 2 Buffware

Core

The vessels had been constructed using the paddle and anvil technique. The color of the paste was generally a reddish beige to tan. The paste had a medium texture and was not very dense.

Temper

Rolled particles of quartz sand formed the major component of the temper. The source of this material was probably a stream bed, as the particles were well rounded. Less frequent were particles of dark, opaque rock, which in one case were fragments of schist. Some sherd temper was present but less frequently than in the Type 1 material. The sherd temper appeared as reddish inclusions, occasionally with temper material of their own. Overall temper was relatively fine and of low volume, making up less than one-quarter of the sherds.

Fracture

The sherds tended to crumble when broken, due to the granular character of the paste.

Surface

Exterior surfaces were smoothed and polished. There was no indication of a wash or other prepared coating. The color of the surface reflected the coloration of the paste, ranging from tan to reddish beige. As a result of polishing on both the interior and exterior, the surface was finely finished and quite hard and resisted erosion well.

Forms

Both bowl and jar forms were present in the sample. The few rim sherds observed represented relatively shallow vessels with direct rims. The jars varied considerably in size. A number of examples possessed a modified shoulder that had a cycle of 45°, similar to the shoulder characteristics of some late Sedentary Hohokam buffware jars. It was not the high shoulder form known from the Patayan I period.

Decoration

A few recovered bowl sherds showed vestiges of a medium to light red paint on the surface. None of the vessels retained enough pigment to permit identification of the motifs involved.

Type 3 Buffware

Core

Construction apparently had been by paddle and anvil. None of the sherds exhibited deep anvil impressions, but several had a series of shallow indentations. Paste ranged from medium gray to light buff in color and tended to be quite coarse in texture. Parting planes were observed in a few sherds, suggesting an incomplete welding of the clay during manufacture. A number of sherds also had inclusions of a soft, white material, probably calcium carbonate.

Temper

The tempering material was quite similar to that observed in plainware Type A sherds, dominated by rolled, clear quartz sand. Lesser quantities of subangular material, principally quartz and feldspar, were also present. A few specimens had small, opaque particles that appeared to be pieces of micaceous schist. Considerable variation in temper was characteristic of this type, but sherd temper was never present. Temper normally accounted for approximately 50% of the volume of the paste.

Walls

Vessel walls were relatively thick, particularly in jar sherds, which averaged 7.5 mm. The thickness of bowl sherds was consistently less.

Fracture

Fracture was variable but generally quite crumbly.

Surface

Surface color ranged from brownish tan to cream. The latter appeared to have resulted from the application of a buff-colored wash or weak slip. This feature tended to appear most frequently on those sherds having a light buff paste. With the exception of a pale cream-colored wash observed on a few sherds, jar interiors showed no surface modification; it is likely that these sherds came from near the necks of vessels. Overall surface finish tended to be relatively coarse, with temper showing through the vessel surface, even on those specimens with the applied slip or wash. Surfaces were unpolished but appeared to have been wiped, possibly with a cloth.

Forms

Both jars and bowls were represented in the sample, which was dominated by sherds from a single pot break recovered from the Flatiron Site (127 of the 233 sherds). Discounting this vessel, jar sherds still predominated in the assemblage, but no jar rims were recovered. The bowls represented all had direct rims and squared-off rim profiles.

Decoration

Two recovered sherds had traces of red paint. In one case, the sherd was so small that nothing could be said about the character of the design. The other sherd had come from a shouldered jar with the design extending along the edge of the shoulder. Once again, little could be said about the overall character of the design, although it appeared to have been a broad painted area with a scalloped lower margin, an execution often seen on large Sedentary period Hohokam shouldered jars.

Redwares

Three types of redware were identified: Sacaton Red, a Hohokam type dated to the Sedentary period (A.D. 900 to 1075+), and two local types. The latter types appeared to have been produced by the application of a red slip to the surface of a locally produced type. In the case of Type R1 redware, a slip was applied to Type D plainware. The applied pigment was a thick, true red slip with a Munsell value of 10R 4/6. The second locally produced redware, Type R2, was characterized by an application of a much thinner layer of pigment or wash over the surface of Type A plainware and Type 1 buffware vessels. The color of the wash ranged from a color similar to that described for Type R1 to a deep reddish brown with a Munsell value of 5YR 3/4. Generally, this material was quite fugitive.

Other Ceramics

Two partial vessels were recovered that represented types associated with regions to the north. The first was an Aquarius Brown jar recovered from the surface of AZ T:5:10(ASM) that comprised the entire ceramic sample from this site. Aquarius Brown is part of the Tizon Brown Ware tradition, a group of series associated with the Upland Yuman cultures, perhaps the Yavapai, who had occupied the region during the Historic period. The dating associated with the type is extremely broad, however, ranging from as early as A.D. 900 to A.D. 1890 (Euler and Dobyns 1958).

The other type recovered was a bowl of Verde Black-on-gray. This type is associated with the Prescott tradition of the upper Verde River and may represent contact with that region. The type is dated between A.D. 1050 and A.D. 1200 (Breternitz 1966), which would agree well with the dates attributed to the later portion of the Sedentary period of the Hohokam. As previously mentioned, Hohokam material dating to this period was also recovered from the Flatiron Site.

Site Assemblages

AZ T:5:9(ASM)

Two sherds were recovered during the investigations at AZ T:5:9(ASM). The specimens appeared to be from the same vessel, a Type 1 buffware jar. This type appears to be in the Patayan tradition, with sherd temper and a dense paste. One sherd was recovered from the surface of Feature 4 and the other from the general site surface approximately 36 m to the west. Little can be said regarding the significance of these pieces, other than that they probably reflected a prehistoric use of the site. The pieces fell within the range of types defined from specimens recovered at the Flatiron Site, where similar specimens were recovered in association with Hohokam Buff Wares.

AZ T:5:10(ASM)

The entire ceramic assemblage recovered at this site consisted of 169 sherds from a single Aquarius Brown vessel, a plainware type associated with the Tizon tradition (Euler and Dobyns 1958). The vessel was a jar with a low shoulder and, apparently, a wide mouth. No rim sherds were recovered, although most of the base and lower portions of the sides were found.

This was the only occurrence of Tizon Brown Ware in the project collections. The project area is considered to be part of the historic Yavapai territory, and it may be that this material represented an occupation that postdated those of the other sites in the current project sample. Unfortunately, the dates associated with the manufacture of Aquarius Brown encompass such a broad span of time that this cannot be proven on the basis of the ceramics alone.

AZ T:5:11(ASM)

Only 24 sherds were recovered from AZ T:5:11(ASM) (Table 5.2). Despite the relatively small size of the sample, considerable diversity was present. Temper ranged from crushed rock (possibly granite or gneiss) to a fine, rolled sand temper associated with Type C plainware sherds. The material occurred in three discrete areas at the site. The buffware occurred in association with Feature 1, the two rock piles in the southern portion of the site. However, all sherds were recovered from the surface of the feature; thus, the association is not well established. The eight sherds appeared to represent a single vessel, probably a bowl; one rim section was distorted in a manner similar to that seen on deep scoops. The interior surface had been highly polished to the point of producing a floated slip. The other two areas were in the northeast portion of the site area. A single plainware sherd was found in association with Feature 12, again recovered from the surface of the unit. The only Hohokam material in the sample, a Wingfield Plain sherd, was found in the unit to the northwest of Feature 12.

Table 5.2. Ceramics Recovered from AZ T:5:11(ASM).

Type	Feature Number			Total
	1	12	General Surface	
Buffware				
Type 3	8			8
Plainware				
Type A		1	5	6
Type C			2	2
Type E			7	7
Wingfield				
Plain			1	1
Total	8	1	15	24

The greatest concentration of material was in the northeast portion of the site, where 14 sherds represented four or five different vessels. Three different types of plainware were represented in the sample. Five of the pieces were Type A, representing fragments of both a jar and a bowl; a single sherd was Type C; and seven sherds were Type E. The latter appeared to have been derived from two vessels, although a single jar with considerable variation in the thickness of the wall would have accounted for the differences. This was the only occurrence of this type in the project sample.

AZ T:5:12(ASM)

During the investigations at AZ T:5:12(ASM), the Flatiron Site, 1,985 sherds were recovered (Table 5.3). The great majority (94.8%) of this sample was recovered during systematic surface collection. The assemblage proved to be a mix of several ceramic traditions, including Hohokam and Patayan buffwares. The collection was dominated, however, by a series of plainware types that appeared to have been locally produced.

Hohokam Buff Ware sherds were mostly Sacaton Red-on-buff, a ceramic type diagnostic of the Sedentary period in the Salt and middle Gila valleys. The buffware sherds were distributed across the site surface with some concentration in the northeastern region of the site in Loci A and B. Several features in this area also produced Hohokam Buff Ware ceramics.

In general, features were largely devoid of diagnostic ceramics. Occupation Surface 1 (Features 45, 100, 106, and 107) produced the majority of temporally sensitive ceramics, including five of the six sherds of Sacaton Red-on-buff recovered from excavated contexts. The sixth sherd was recovered from Feature 28, an eroded roasting pit to the south of the occupation surface. All of the identified sherds were from jar forms, and at least two vessels appeared to be represented. The sherds from Feature 107 appeared to have been from a single vessel with a modified shoulder and a hatchured, undulating design, which might have been a snake motif. The second vessel was represented by sherds recovered from the occupation surface and a pit associated with it (Feature 45). The design appeared to have been a series of scrolls with an offset panel of bordered fringe.

Lower Colorado Buff Ware types were also present in the assemblage. These materials bore an affinity to the Lower Gila Series defined by Schroeder (1958). The current sample, however, appeared to contain some variants of Schroeder types that may have been locally produced. This appeared to be the case with Type 3, a buffware that seemed to be related to the dominant plainware at the site. Other Patayan-like ceramics were present in the site sample, although in lower frequencies. Several sherds exhibited a red wash applied to the exterior surface. Lower Colorado Buff Ware was concentrated in the central and southern loci of the site (Loci D and E) within this area. Buffware sherds were widely dispersed, with one notable exception at Feature 90, a surface concentration consisting of over 127 Type 3 sherds representing a single jar.

Painted decorations were observed on 13 sherds, but only one specimen had sufficient paint remaining to allow recognition of the design. This sherd appeared to have been a piece of a Palomas Red-on-buff bowl.

Plainwares accounted for 71% of the sample recovered. A sand-tempered type (Type 1 plainware) that appeared to be of local origin dominated the plainware assemblage (82%). These sherds were widely distributed across the site, with all of the loci containing this material. Locus E and the southern portion of Locus C, along with the surrounding areas, had a somewhat greater percentage of this type than was found in other areas. There were, however, some isolated concentrations, which probably represented pot breaks. Generally, this type was less well represented in the southeastern part of Locus D, which bordered the main channel of Fourmile Wash.

Table 5.3. Ceramics Recovered from the Flatiron Site (AZ T:5:12, ASM)

Ceramic Types	Feature Number																					Total
	Excavation Unit											Surface Collection										
	3	28	45	71	85	103	106	107	109	111	Others	2	3	19	31	33	90	91	97	107	GS*	
Decorated																						
Hohokam																						
Sacaton R/B	1		2					1	2							2			1		22	31
Santa Cruz R/B																			1			1
Sac./S.C. R/B					1																	1
Unidentified R/B		5																1			18	24
Patayan																						
Palomas R/B																					1	1
Type 1																					2	2
Type 2																					6	6
Type 3																					4	4
Buffware																						
Hohokam	3		2										1						4		96	106
Patayan																						
Type 1	5		1							2	1		2								21	32
Type 2			2																		71	73
Type 3	1		1			2					1						127				73	205
Unidentified																					13	13
Redware																						
Sacaton Red																					6	6
Type R1																					6	6
Type R2														4							26	30
Unidentified redware																					2	2

Table 5.3. Ceramics Recovered from the Flatiron Site (AZ T:5:12, ASM), continued

Ceramic Type	Feature Number											Surface Collection										Total
	Excavation Unit																					
	3	28	45	71	85	103	106	107	109	111	Others	2	3	19	31	33	90	91	97	107	GS*	
Plainware																						
Wingfield																					25	25
Gila Plain			1																		44	45
Type A		3	9	6	1	9	12		8		16	2	16	3	10	1	32	3		13	1019	1163
Type B						1					2				4		2				105	114
Type C																					13	13
Type D			1												1						52	54
Intrusive																						
Prescott Gray																					28	28
Unidentified whiteware																					1	1
Totals	2	17	18	6	2	12	13	2	8	4	20	4	19	3	15	3	129	33	9	13	1654	1986

*General Surface

A second type (Type B) accounted for 8% of the plainware assemblage. There was a major concentration of this type in the southeastern area of Locus D, with 57% of the type occurring in a single area. A second, minor concentration of material occurred in the area of Feature 109, an occupation surface with an associated pit in the northern portion of Locus D.

The remaining plainware types, including Wingfield Plain, Types C and D of the local traditions, and Gila Plain, Gila Variety, occurred in limited numbers and were distributed widely across the site with no apparent concentrations. Wingfield Plain is generally associated with the Hohokam occupation of the Salt River drainage and the northern periphery of the Hohokam sphere of influence. This is the dominant plainware type recovered from sites excavated along New River (Doyel and Elson 1985:453), and it is commonly recovered in the Salt River basin (Crown 1981:94–97). Gila Plain, Gila Variety occurs in lower frequency in the Salt River basin but is present in abundance in assemblages from sites in the Gila River drainage (Crown 1981:97; Weaver 1974:115).

The other intrusive ceramics included a concentration of Prescott Gray Ware sherds in Locus E. These appeared to represent the remains of a single Verde Black-on-gray bowl. A single undecorated whiteware sherd, presumably from northern Arizona, was also recovered from the site surface.

Overall, there were a greater number of jar than bowl sherds in the sample. Jars accounted for over 78% of the identifiable forms. With the exception of a single sherd from the rim of a deep scoop, the remaining 22% were bowls. With respect to rims, this relationship was reversed, with jar forms accounting for only 41% of the sample. This is not unusual; bowls, by nature, will produce more rim surface for the volume of container. The overall dominance of jar forms may be a reflection of an emphasis on storage and related activities. Unfortunately, few sherds were large enough to permit estimates of vessel size except in a general sense. The assemblage appeared to include a number of large, thick-walled vessels that may well have been used for storage of food or water. For example, one rim sherd of the Type 1 buffware had an estimated diameter of over 19 cm.

The Flatiron Site appeared to have been occupied by a population with ties to the Patayan populations of the southwestern portions of Arizona and to a lesser extent with nearby Hohokam groups. The technology of the locally produced ceramics showed the strongest affinity to Lower Colorado Buff Ware manufactured along the lower Gila rather than to materials originating along the Colorado River. The similarities appeared to be the strongest with the Lower Gila Series (Schroeder 1958), a tradition generally dated from A.D. 1150 into the historic period. The presence of the Verde Black-on-gray bowl in the assemblage also suggested this temporal assignment, as it is a type dated between A.D. 1050 and 1200 (Breternitz 1966).

The recovery of one sherd of Santa Cruz Red-on-buff suggested the possibility of earlier activities at the site, perhaps during the late ninth century A.D., while the design style suggested a late Colonial period placement; but little weight can be put on this single specimen. The Sedentary period material was proportionately better represented. The conventional dates attributed to Sacaton Red-on-buff and Sacaton Red would overlap the dates suggested for the Verde Black-on-gray and Lower Colorado Buff Ware material.

AZ T:5:17(ASM)

The sample from AZ T:5:17(ASM) was the second largest from project sites, with 216 sherds representing eight types. Lower Colorado Buff Ware (Table 5.4) accounted for 178 sherds, or 82.4%

Table 5.4. Ceramics Recovered from AZ T:5:17(ASM)

Ceramic Type	Feature Number						Total
	1	2	3	4	5	GS*	
Hohokam Buff Ware			1				1
Patayan Type 1	36	55	4	3	2	3	103
Patayan Type 2			46		21		67
Patayan Type 3		4		2	2		8
Redware Type 2		1	8				9
Plainware Type A	1	5	7	5	3	2	23
Plainware Type C					3		3
Wingfield Plain					1		1
Unidentifiable		1					1
Total	37	66	66	10	32	5	216

*General Surface

of the sample. A single Hohokam Buff Ware sherd and one sherd of Wingfield Plain were identified during the analysis. Unfortunately, the buffware sherds were too eroded to have retained any paint, and no temporal assignment could be made. The remainder of the assemblage was composed of Lower Colorado Buff Ware with a red slip applied to the vessel exteriors and plainwares that appeared to have been locally produced.

The buffwares were dominated by Types 1 and 2. Within these designations there is a certain amount of variability. Type 1, characterized by sherd and rolled quartz sand temper, varies in the relative quantity of these components as well as the quantity of the tempering material in the sherd. Type 2 is characterized by the presence of rolled quartz sand temper and the absence of sherd temper. This type resembles a number of the Type 1 sherds in other characteristics and may represent no more than a variant of that type. Both of these types were expressed in relatively finely made vessels averaging about 4 mm in thickness. Only a few rim sherds were recovered from the site, the majority from a single vessel associated with Feature 2. This rim was unique in the project sample in that there was an encircling filleted design impressed into both surfaces of the edges. Such filleting is described as occurring on Parker Buff, a type within the Lower Colorado Buff Ware Series described by Schroeder (1958). The third buffware also has rolled quartz sand temper, but the temper particles are generally much larger and coarser in texture, although considerable variability exists.

The redware sherds present in the sample appeared to be examples of Type 1 buffware that had had a red slip applied to the vessel exterior. At most, two vessels were represented, with the eight sherds recovered from Feature 3 probably derived from a single vessel. The slip was orange-red in color.

The plainware ceramics composed the second largest subset of the sample, with 27 specimens. The majority fell within the range of Type A. These specimens tended to be thinner, with a paste that had a finer texture than the majority of the specimens recovered at the Flatiron Site. The other types observed at the Flatiron Site included three sherds of Type C and a single sherd of Wingfield Plain.

Although this sample was relatively small, several observations can be made. The high incidence of Lower Colorado Buff Ware and the near absence of Hohokam material suggested that the local population was interacting with the former to a far greater degree. Unfortunately, the sample contained no temporally diagnostic ceramics; therefore, the site could not be placed within the regional temporal framework. Although many of the sherds fell within the range of ceramic types recovered at the Flatiron Site, subtle differences between the two samples suggested that although these communities had been part of the same tradition, they may not have derived from the same immediate population.

Summary and Conclusions

The majority of the ceramic assemblage appeared to have been locally produced, suggesting that the population inhabiting the region had been distinct from neighboring groups. Given the other ceramic traditions represented, the populations that had occupied this area (with the possible exception of AZ T:5:10, ASM) appear to have been more closely related to the producers of Lower Colorado Buff Ware than to Hohokam groups. The makers of Hohokam ceramics appear to have been intrusive. It is possible, but unlikely, that these sherds represented a minor but discrete occupation. In general, the ceramics indicated a local tradition that had absorbed traits and received vessels from the neighboring cultural traditions. This would, for instance, explain the occurrence of local redwares when this technology had been largely dropped by the main Patayan groups around A.D. 1000 (Waters 1982:287).

LITHICS

Flaked Stone Artifacts

Gary Funkhouser

This section provides a descriptive analysis of the 1,304 flaked stone artifacts recovered during the Fourmile Wash Project. The assemblage included 31 formal tools and retouched flakes, 177 cores, and 1,096 pieces of debitage. Although these materials were collected from five of the eight project sites, the majority were retrieved from AZ T:5:11(ASM) and AZ T:5:12(ASM), the Flatiron Site. A general typology for the project lithic assemblage is presented in Table 5.5.

Debitage

The 1,096 pieces of debitage recovered during the project accounted for 84% of the total lithic assemblage. There were 407 (37.1%) complete flakes, 556 (50.7%) flake fragments, and 133 (12.1%) pieces of shatter. The distribution of debitage by site location is shown in Table 5.6.

Table 5.5. Lithics from the Fourmile Wash Project

Site (ASM)	Debitage		Cores		Tools		Total
	N	%	N	%	N	%	
AZ T:5:8	17	45.9	16	43.2	4	10.8	37
AZ T:5:9	14	66.7	6	28.6	1	4.8	21
AZ T:5:11	192	88.3	20	9.3	4	1.8	216
AZ T:5:12	817	85.4	123	12.8	17	1.8	957
AZ T:5:17	56	76.7	12	16.4	5	6.8	73
Total	**1096**		**177**		**31**		**1304**

Table 5.6. Debitage from Project Sites

Site (ASM)	Complete Flakes		Flake Fragments		Shatter		Total	Use Wear	
	N	%	N	%	N	%		N	%
AZ T:5:8	8	47.1	9	52.9	0	0.0	17	0	0.0
AZ T:5:9	4	28.6	9	64.3	1	7.1	14	0	0.0
AZ T:5:11	41	21.3	118	61.5	33	17.2	192	15	7.8
AZ T:5:12	344	42.1	385	47.1	88	10.8	817	104	12.7
AZ T:5:17	10	17.9	35	62.5	11	19.6	56	0	0.0
Total	**407**		**556**		**133**		**1096**	**119**	

The debitage category includes complete flakes, flake fragments, and shatter. Any flake that had its striking platform and distal and lateral edges intact was classified as a complete flake. Any flake that had identifiable interior and exterior surfaces but was missing one or more of its proximal, distal, or lateral edges was classified as a flake fragment. Any piece of flaked stone for which the interior surface could not be discerned was defined as shatter.

Sullivan and Rozen (1985) have suggested that core reduction strategies should yield a high number of complete flakes and shatter and that a high percentage of flake fragments might be indicative of tool manufacture. The data from the present study are not strictly comparable with theirs, however, so the observations possible are limited.

The overall pattern of a relatively high frequency of cores and a low frequency of formal tools (relative to the debitage collection) suggested a pattern of core reduction and use of flakes without further modification. Once flakes had been produced from cores, little effort had been expended in tool manufacture.

Utilized Flakes

Flakes with a clear pattern of wear damage (not accidental breakage or damage) along one or more of the edges were classified as showing use. Wear damage was defined as a pattern of three or more contiguous unifacial flake scars. Most of the 119 artifacts exhibiting use wear appeared to have been used as scrapers or for cutting purposes.

An even greater number of the flakes probably had been utilized but did not show the evidence required for classification. Many of the flakes were naturally damaged from surface exposure. Also, it is harder to visually establish patterns of use wear on medium- and coarse-grained materials such as those from the project assemblage than it is on fine-grained specimens. Two of the basalt flakes from AZ T:5:12(ASM) may have been removed in the process of shaping metates.

Tools and Retouched Flakes

Thirty-one tools and retouched flakes were recovered during the project. The most common tool types were scraper planes, scrapers, and notched pieces. The overall pattern of tool manufacture appeared to have been one of expedience and simplicity.

A unifacially retouched obsidian flake and three scrapers were recovered from AZ T:5:8(ASM). Two of the scrapers were made of obsidian, while the third was made of chalcedony. A quartz scraper/hammerstone was recovered from the Flatiron Site. Two notched pieces and one scraper, all made of rhyolite, and one nondiagnostic triangular obsidian projectile point came from AZ T:5:11(ASM). From AZ T:5:12(ASM) there were five scraper-planes, three scrapers, four notched pieces, two choppers, two drills, and one bifacially retouched flake. Three scrapers, one retouched flake, and one obsidian point were recovered from AZ T:5:17(ASM). The point was small and triangular with a straight base. Two of the scrapers were made of fine chert and had been extensively retouched. The morphology and craftsmanship evidenced by these specimens may indicate a limited Archaic occupation.

Cores and Hammerstones

The summary figures for cores and core fragments are shown in Table 5.7. In general, it appeared that local cobbles had been used as raw material. The high percentage of rhyolite/andesite was consistent with the debitage data. The overall pattern appeared to have been one of use of naturally occurring cobbles to produce flakes through simple hard hammer percussion.

Eleven of the cores showed evidence of battering and had probably also been used as hammerstones. Three cobble hammerstones were also recovered. Two of these (one made of rhyolite/andesite and one made of quartzite) were recovered from the Flatiron Site. One quartzite cobble hammerstone was recovered from AZ T:5:11(ASM). The cobble hammerstones had probably been used like the core/hammerstones, to produce flakes through percussion or to shape ground stone artifacts.

Table 5.7. Cores from Project Sites by Material Type

Site (ASM)	R/A		Obs		Cha		Qzt		Che		Vba		Qua		Bas		Total
	N	%	N	%	N	%	N	%	N	%	N	%	N	%	N	%	
AZ T:5:8	4	25.0	12	75.0													16
AZ T:5:9	2	33.3			1	16.7	1	16.7	1	16.7			1	16.7			6
AZ T:5:11	13	65.0	4	20.0					1	5.0	1	5.0			1	5.0	20
AZ T:5:12	95	77.3	8	6.5	5	4.1	7	5.7	4	3.2	1	0.8	2	1.6	1	0.8	123
AZ T:5:17	2	16.7	5	41.7	2	16.7					2	16.7	1	8.3			12
Total	116		29		8		8		6		4		4		2		177

R/A - Rhyolite/Andesite
Che - Chert
Obs - Obsidian
Vba - Vesicular Basalt
Cha - Chalcedony
Qua - Quartz
Qzt - Quartzite
Bas - Basalt

Raw Material Types

Eight material types were identified in the lithic assemblage. The rhyolite/andesite category accounted for almost 60% of the entire sample, with chalcedony (8.1%) and quartzite (7.2%) occurring as relatively common material types. Table 5.8 shows material type distribution by site.

The obsidian recovered occurred in the form of small nodules or nodule fragments. These nodules, commonly referred to as Apache tears, occur naturally in desert pavement situations within the project area. Huckell (1979) has noted that the small size of Apache tears necessitates a specialized flaking technique known as bipolar reduction. Using this method, a nodule is placed on an anvil and then struck with a hammerstone. Flakes produced in this manner tend to be thick and irregularly shaped. As would be expected, they also show evidence of crushing or battering at both ends. Because of the small size of the nodules and the relative inefficiency of bipolar reduction, the cores are usually totally exhausted.

For the rest of the material, the pattern also seemed to be use of locally available materials. Except for two chert scrapers recovered from AZ T:5:17(ASM), all of the material seemed to be local. Rhyolite/andesite cobbles are abundant in the wash channels of the area and are a good source of medium- to coarse-grained flaking material.

Site Assemblages

Due to the size and relative complexity of the Flatiron Site (AZ T:5:12, ASM), investigators felt that it might be a profitable place to examine intrasite variability within the lithic assemblage. Lithic materials from the site were separated into categories that included general surface collection, Locus D, Locus E, and surface features.

Researchers then attempted to determine if any of the lithic materials from the spatially associated features, thought to represent discrete activity areas, might vary in form or frequency from those of the general site collection. The attempt was not fruitful because of the small sample sizes recovered from these proveniences, the largest being 26 pieces of debitage. Even when considered as a single sample and compared against the other site proveniences, the feature lithics were not strikingly different. Overall, the features tended to have a slightly inflated number of flake fragments and shatter, but this higher frequency of smaller-sized materials may have resulted from the more intensive collection efforts around features. The frequencies of raw material types were comparable with those from the rest of the site as well.

Conclusion

In general, the lithic technology represented by the flaked stone collection from the Fourmile Wash Project sites was characterized by the expedient production of flakes and simple tools. The general technology seems to have been simple hard hammer percussion. Flakes tended to have simple, unprepared platforms and prominent bulbs of percussion. There was little evidence of retouch or other intentional modification of flakes once they had been extracted from a core.

The only exceptions to this were two finely made chert scrapers from AZ T:5:17(ASM) that were unique in both material and extent of modification. They may have represented an Archaic component, although no other evidence in the flaked stone collection suggested this.

Table 5.8. Raw Material Types within Project Lithic Assemblageb

Artifact Type	R/A		Obs		Cha		Qzt		Che		Vra		Qua		Bas		Total
	N	%	N	%	N	%	N	%	N	%	N	%	N	%	N	%	
Debitage	730		72		94		79		53		47		18		3		1096
Core	116		29		8		8		6		4		4		2		177
Tools	17		6		4		1		2				1				31
Total	863	66.2	107	8.2	106	8.1	88	6.7	61	4.7	51	3.9	23	1.8	5	0.4	1304

R/A - Rhyolite/Andesite   Obs - Obsidian   Cha - Chalcedony   Qzt - Quartzite
Che - Chert   Vba - Vesicular Basalt   Qua - Quartz   Bas - Basalt

Ground Stone Artifacts

Arthur W. Vokes

The Flatiron Site (AZ T:5:12, ASM)

During the investigations at the Flatiron Site, 21 pieces of ground stone were collected. The assemblage included 12 manos, 3 metates, and 6 other specimens, including a fragment of a stone "doughnut" and 2 small pendant fragments. The majority of these specimens were recovered from the surface of the site (Table 5.9).

Manos

Eight of the manos were otherwise unmodified cobbles. In conventional typologies, these specimens fell within the class of grinding implements termed simple handstones. Six of them had one grinding surface. In the other two cases, minimal to moderate grinding was present on the second grinding surface. The ends of three specimens were battered, apparently as a result of their use as pounding implements.

Four additional specimens exhibited some degree of edge modification, suggesting that the makers had attempted to create a more formal grinding stone, so these artifacts conformed to the criteria used to distinguish manos from handstones (Haury 1976:281). The edges of the rock had been pecked by a hammerstone and then ground, resulting in a subrectangular shape. In contrast to the unshaped handstones, all of these specimens possessed multiple grinding surfaces. One was unusual in that the two grinding surfaces were contiguous, separated by a sharply defined angular boundary. This specimen was granitic in composition and had been extensively used. On the other specimens, the two grinding surfaces were in opposition to each other. Only one of the specimens was large enough (18.6 cm in length) to suggest that it might have required the use of both hands. This was also the most formally shaped specimen in the collection.

The dominant material represented in the collection was basalt, accounting for over half of the recovered specimens. All of these had some vesicles present; however, only two specimens could be characterized as vesicular basalt. Other forms of igneous rock accounted for two additional specimens. Of the remaining three items, two were made from quartzite and one from a poorly consolidated rock that appeared to be sandstone.

With one exception, the specimens from the Flatiron Site exhibited moderate to heavy use, suggesting that they employed over a period of time. Whether this use had been continuous or intermittent could not be determined.

Metates

Three metates were recovered. One was a complete shallow trough metate open at one end. It was largely unshpaed, and its form suggested that it would not have sat upright without additional support. Areas of pecking and patterned flaking suggested that some efforts had been made to shape the metate; however, these areas were not extensive. A second specimen, in the early stages of use, was also irregularly shaped. The grinding surface was flat with limited areas of pecking and showed only high-point grinding. The piece had been shattered from heat exposure. The final specimen was a fragmentary section of a metate. The original form was difficult to determine, although it definitely had a shallow central depression, suggesting a basin form; but the fragment also could have been the closed end of a shallow trough metate. All of these specimens were manufactured from igneous rock, two from basalt and the third from an unidentified material.

Table 5.9. Ground Stone Artifacts from the Flatiron Site (AZ T:5:12, ASM)

Feature	Provenience	St/L[1]	Artifact	Material	C/F[2]	GS[3]	Comments	Measurements Length	Width	Thickness
0	N150 W200	surface (50 x 50)	handstone	andesite	C	1	light use, ends battered	11.5	6.7	5.9
0	N210 W100	surface (10 x 25)	handstone	basalt	F	2	1 heavy use, 1 light use	-	-	-
0	N316 W154	surface	handstone	basalt?	C	1	heavy use	11.5	8.2	6.3
0	N410 E150	surface	handstone	vesicular basalt	C	1	moderate use	9.1	6.2	5.2
0	N580 E15	surface (10 x 30)	handstone	sandstone?	C	1	moderate use	13.6	9.0	5.1
0	N580 E15	surface (10 x 30)	handstone	vesicular basalt	C	1	heavy use	11.9	9.3	8.8
0	N580 E15	surface (10 x 30)	handstone	quartzite	C	2	both heavily used, shaped	14.4	9.1	4.9
0	N850 E250	surface	mano/handstone	granite	C	2	contiguous ground surfaces - both heavily used, shaped	14.3	9.5	7.7
0	N950 E200	surface (50 x 50)	handstone	quartzite	C	1	heavily used	15.8	10.6	5.8
0	Trench 25	backdirt	mano	basalt	C	2	1 heavy use, 1 moderate use, shaped	18.6	8.8	6.0
111	N536.2 E1004.57	mbd[4]	handstone	basalt	C	2	1 heavy use, 1 moderate use, burned	12.0	11.2	5.7
0	N410 E75	surface (10 x 25)	flat grinding stone	unidentified igneous	R[5]	1	pecked/ground, very light use	19.5	12.0	9.7
0	N580 E15	surface (10 x 30)	basin/shallow trough metate	basalt	F	1	use of natural depression, high point grinding (large flake removed from edge-core)	-	-	-
103	N596.3 E11.8	St. 50	trough metate	basalt	C	1	trough, shallow, shaped	46.0	23.9	17.3

[1]Stratum/Level
[2]Complete/Fragment
[3]Grinding Surfaces
[4]Meters Below Datum
[5]Reconstructible

Other Ground Stone

Six additional ground stone artifacts were recovered from the site. Four were formally shaped objects: a stone doughnut, a pestle, and two pendant fragments. The other two items were a piece of schist that appeared to have been shaped and a fragment that, although ground, was too small to permit identification of the original form.

Approximately one-third of the doughnut remained. The function of these artifacts has been the subject of speculation for many years, and no satisfactory explanation has as yet been offered. They are known from numerous archaeological sites in southern Arizona, including Snaketown (Haury 1950:332–34) and the Cashion Site (Antieau and Greenwald 1981:192). The pestle was a small, rectangular block of basalt that had been shaped by removing a series of large flakes, leaving only a small area of the natural cortex. One end of the block had been rounded through grinding and battering. Several other corners appeared to have had some battering as well but had not been ground. The ground area did not extend up the sides of the piece, suggesting that the mortar employed probably had been quite shallow.

A tabular piece of schist was recovered from the surface of the site. The specimen was irregularly shaped, and there were several areas of possible high-point grinding across the surfaces. In addition, the sections along the edges may have been ground.

Two pieces of shaped argillite also were recovered from the Flatiron Site, both fragments of carved and ground pendants. One specimen seemed to be part of a perched bird form with the wings drawn close to the body, viewed from the front. Unfortunately, only the central portion of the body remained, as the head and tail segments had been broken off. The remains of a perforation for suspension were visible along one of the breaks. The second piece might have been from a geometric pendant, also broken through the perforation. On the latter specimen the perforation was equidistant from the three remaining sides, suggesting that the original pendant may have had a square or rectangular form. This second piece was quite a bit thinner than the bird-shaped specimen, indicating that the two fragments represented two different artifacts.

AZ T:5:8(ASM)

Two pieces of ground stone were recovered during the intensive surface collection of AZ T:5:8(ASM), both apparently fragments of metates. Although both fragments were made from vesicular basalt, the coloration and texture of the rock indicated that they had not originated from the same artifact. The specific form of metate represented could not be positively determined in either case; one of the specimens may have been basin-shaped.

AZ T:5:9(ASM)

Eleven pieces of ground stone were collected during the intensive surface collection of this site (Table 5.10). The dominant artifacts were handstones, which were cobbles that were generally unmodified except for the grinding area. All of the specimens at the site were made from igneous rocks, basalt being the dominant material. Only one of the specimens possessed more than one grinding surface, and only one showed any evidence of efforts to shape the overall form.

AZ T:5:11(ASM)

A single complete handstone was recovered from this site. The specimen was an irregularly shaped piece of granitic rock with two grinding surfaces. One of the surfaces had been partially

Table 5.10. Ground Stone Artifacts from AZ T:5:9(ASM)

Feature	Provenience	St/L[1]	Artifact	Material	C/F[2]	GS[3]	Comments
0	N134 E58	surface	handstone	unidentified igneous	F	1	
0	N136 E62	surface	handstone	basalt?	C	1	
0	N142 E126	surface	handstone	vesicular basalt	C	2	1 side w/high point, 1 heavily ground
0	N144 E112	surface	handstone	granite	F	1	
0	N150 E42	surface	metate (form unk)	vesicular basalt	F	1	
0	N152 E38	surface	handstone	granite	F	2	1 ground surface may have been used after fragmentation
0	N160 E110	surface	ground stone (unk)	poor granite	F	1	high point ground
4	N128 E76	surface	handstone	granite	F	1	
7	N78 E72	surface	handstone	unidentified igneous	F	1	high point ground
7	N90 E80	surface	flat basin metate	basalt	R[4]	2	1 basin ground, 1 flat ground heat fractured
7	N92 E70	surface	handstone (mano)	basalt	F	1	grinding surface, very convex, some shaping

[1]Stratum/Level
[2]Complete/Fragment
[3]Grinding Surfaces
[4]Reconstructible

destroyed by a series of shallow spalls; apparently the opposite surface was utilized after this damage had been inflicted. No effort had been made to modify the form of the handstone; however, two areas of battering were present along the sides.

AZ T:5:14(ASM)

Seven pieces of ground stone were recovered from AZ T:5:14(ASM). The majority of these were small fragments that lacked morphological attributes (Table 5.11). Most of the remaining specimens were handstones. These appeared to have been selected for use because of their natural shape, as none exhibited any evidence of modification and were, therefore, quite irregular in shape. In all but one case, only one surface had been employed for grinding. The exception was a handstone made out of quartzite. One side had been utilized far more extensively than the other,

Table 5.11. Ground Stone Artifacts from AZ T:5:14(ASM)

Feature	Provenience	St/L[1]	Artifact	Material	C/F[2]	GS[3]	Comments
0	N5 W68	surface	handstone	basalt	F	1	
0	N12 W65	surface	unknown form	granite	F	1	
0	N28 W80	surface	handstone	degenerated granite	C	1	
0	N30 W80	surface	handstone	basalt	F	1	limited area
0	N58 W29	surface	unknown form	vesicular basalt	F	1	high point grinding, burned
0	N62 W114	surface	flat metate	rhyolite	C	1	large flakes removed after grinding use
0	N71 W122	surface	handstone	quartzite	F	2	1 surface has limited high point grinding

[1]Stratum/Level
[2]Complete/Fragment
[3]Grinding Surfaces

but both sides appeared to have been employed. The only metate recovered was a relatively small slab that was ground on one face. The grinding was not extensive and was largely limited to the higher projections on the surface.

In general, the technology employed was one of convenience. The grinding implements did not reflect a situation in which makers had undertaken extensive efforts to prepare the tools. The amount of grinding on the working surfaces of most of the specimens suggested their use had been of limited duration.

AZ T:5:17 (ASM)

Seven pieces of ground stone were recovered during the investigations of this site (Table 5.12), including one whole and three fragmentary metates and three grinding stones.

The whole metate was a tabular piece of granite that had been ground on one surface and used as a flat metate. The wear pattern from grinding was restricted to the central portion of the surface and was limited only to the high points. Generally, the metate fragments appeared to have been from flat metates, although one piece was too fragmentary to permit identification of the original form. Only one of the specimens exhibited any evidence of shaping, in this case extensive pecking on the unground face.

Three grinding stones also were recovered. Two were handstones, and the third was a well-formed sandstone mano. The handstones were both made of vesicular basalt. One of these was composed of two fragments recovered from the surface deposits of two separate features (Features 3 and 4, an artifact scatter and a rock concentration). The cause for the dispersal of the fragments was unclear, as neither fragment appeared to have been utilized subsequent to its original breakage. The final specimen was recovered from the fill of Feature 5 and was much more formal in shape, having multiple grinding surfaces. One of the three grinding surfaces was limited primarily to high-point grinding, as if it had seen limited use at the time of disposal. Its appearance was similar to multifaceted specimens recovered from Ventana Cave (Haury 1950:316).

The general trend of the collection suggested a relatively casual use, but the presence of the one multifaceted specimen may represent a more intensive use pattern than was otherwise indicated.

Table 5.12. Ground Stone Artifacts from AZ T:5:17(ASM)

Feature	Provenience	St/L[1]	Artifact	Material	C/F[2]	GS[3]	Comments
1	N56 W57	surface	flat metate	granite	C	1	high point, grinding only
2	N75 W30	surface	flat metate	vesicular basalt	F	1	
2	N78 W35	surface	metate	granite	F	1	possible very shallow trough
3	N84 W4	surface	unknown metate	basalt	F	1	shaped
3	N93 W24	surface	handstone	vesicular basalt	C	1	
3/4	N93 W24 N33 W27	surface	handstone	vesicular basalt	R[4]	1	2 pieces that attach
5	N86.71 W19.41	surface	mano	sandstone	C	3	shaped

[1]Stratum/Level
[2]Complete/Fragment
[3]Grinding Surfaces
[4]Reconstructible

SHELL ARTIFACTS

Arthur W. Vokes

Five pieces of shell were recovered, all from the Flatiron Site. The five pieces probably represented four different artifacts. Two artifacts, a bracelet and a ring, had been manufactured from *Glycymeris*. Approximately half of the bracelet and ring bands remained. The bracelet fragment was part of a plain band that had been ground and polished to give a steep face to the exterior of the band. The band was 5.1 mm wide and 5.7 mm thick, thus falling comfortably within the range suggested for the Type 2 bracelets defined by Haury (1976:313). In contrast, the band of the ring was not as extensively modified. This may have been a reflection of the species employed, *G. multicostata*, which is characterized by pronounced, closely spaced, radial ribs. If left unmodified, these morphological features provide a decorative element. In the case of the ring, the exterior edge had been ground back and steepened, but much of the exterior surface had not been modified, leaving the ribs in relief.

Laevicardium elatum was the species represented in the other three shell artifacts. Two unworked fragments that probably represented a single valve were recovered, along with a fragment of a "perforated shell." This type of artifact manufactured from *L. elatum* is known from a number of Hohokam sites in the Salt and Gila river basins (Haury 1937:146, 1976:316–17) and appears to have been most common during the Sedentary period (Vokes 1984:544).

Although *Glycymeris* and *Laevicardium* are both represented in the biotic communities of the California coast, the most likely source for this material is the Gulf of California. The species of *Glycymeris* large enough to be used in the manufacture of bracelets does not occur in the colder waters off California. Additionally, the northern limit of the species *G. multicostata* is the Gulf of California. The range of *L. elatum* extends northward along the California coast as far as the San Pedro, but it is relatively rare. This species is commonly recovered from Hohokam sites.

6

GEOARCHAEOLOGICAL CONSIDERATIONS

Bruce B. Huckell

This chapter provides a discussion of the geomorphic setting of the project sites and presents observations concerning prehistoric land use in the area, based largely on information obtained from aerial photographs and from one brief visit to the project area. During this visit, investigators examined backhoe trench profiles and noted the surface characteristics of the area.

This study explores those aspects of the local geomorphology that may have particular value in understanding the use of the area by prehistoric human groups. The geomorphic features located within and near the project area have produced a relatively unusual situation that could have been attractive to prehistoric people for at least two reasons: the area's floodwater farming potential and the promotion of annual plant growth in the washes.

REGIONAL CONTEXT

The project area lies just south of an eastern outlier of the Bighorn Mountains known as the Belmont Mountains, approximately 5 miles (8 km) west of the Hassayampa River (Figure 1.1). The Belmont Mountains consist of a core of older Precambrian granite that was broken during the Cretaceous period by intrusive dikes and plugs of rhyolite. Erosion and weathering of these rocks during the Tertiary and Quaternary periods produced a broad alluvial plain. During the Quaternary period, however, this plain was broken by volcanic fissure flows, which stand today as isolated basalt plugs (Wilson et al. 1957). One of these is Flatiron Mountain, which dominates the topography of the project area. Its flat crown stands at a height of approximately 280 feet (86 m) above the surrounding alluvial plain. Viewed from the air, this feature appears as an east-west-oriented, narrow (2.1 x 0.6 km), boat-shaped butte with its stern to the east and its prow to the west. This alignment is perpendicular to the overall trend of the drainages in the area. These ephemeral washes are tributaries of Centennial Wash, which they join approximately 17 miles (27 km) south of Flatiron Mountain (Figure 6.1). Flowing from northwest to southeast, Centennial Wash joins the Gila River approximately 13 miles (21 km) west of Buckeye. At that point the Gila River turns southward to pass between the Buckeye Hills and the Maricopa Mountains on the east and the Gila Bend Mountains on the west.

LOCAL CONTEXT

Flatiron Mountain not only dominates the view in the project area but also exerts a powerful influence on the local geomorphology (Figure 6.1). The surrounding ephemeral washes carry the limited runoff from localized heavy rains across the alluvial plain. Fourmile Wash, the major drainage in the project area, becomes a major channel at the southern foot of Flatiron Mountain. Smaller tributaries of this drainage extend around the western and eastern sides of the mountain.

Although they are not completely separated, these washes basically form two major systems. The eastern system consists of a series of closely spaced channels that drain an ancient alluvial fan surface. The western system flows around the western side of Flatiron Mountain and incorporates much of the area to the north of the mountain as well. The washes in this system show fewer branches and greater integration, forming long, straight channels.

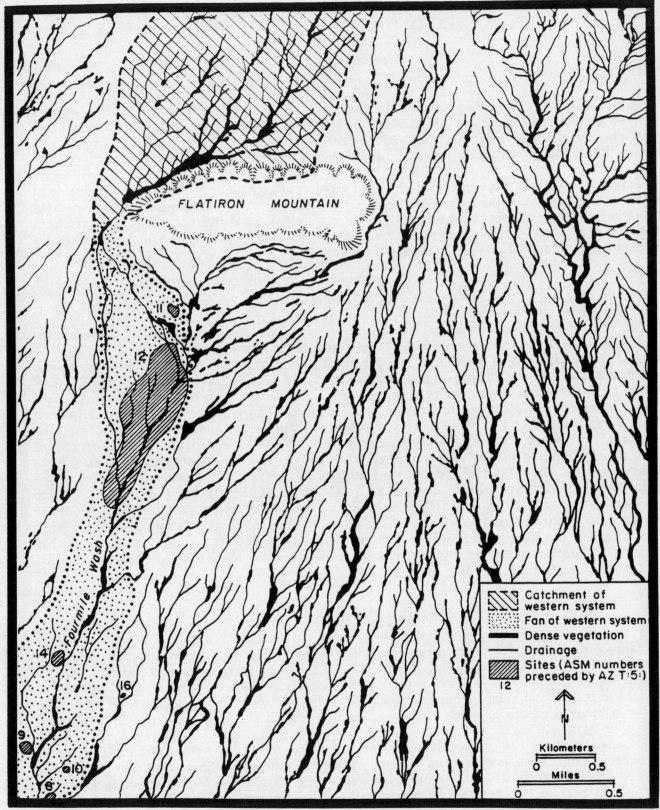

Figure 6.1. Drainage patterns and geomorphological features in the vicinity of Flatiron Mountain.

The eastern system drains a geomorphic surface that is older than that drained by the western system. This surface is composed of relatively well developed desert pavements with strong to moderate coatings of desert varnish. Along the streams in this eastern system, discrete, linear concentrations of vegetation occur, varying in length from a few tens of meters to as much as 100 m in the channel bottoms. Investigators visited one of these habitats, approximately 300 m south of the foot of Flatiron Mountain. The area consisted of a very dense stand of trees, shrubs, and grasses located in the central fork of Fourmile Wash. This lush community included large blue palo verdes, ironwoods, hackberries, and mesquites, with an understory of bursage (near the margins), thornbush, graythorn, various annuals, and grasses. No distinct channel was present in this area, and investigators concluded from examining the bases of the trees that deposition was an active, ongoing process: neither the roots nor the basal swellings of the roots were visible.

Assuming that this pattern of vegetation can serve as a basis for generalization, these small riparian associations are probably the result of a simple positive feedback relationship between runoff and plants. That is, runoff flowing down the wash channels might encounter an obstacle of some sort (a gravel bar, a large branch, a large shrub, or a tree), causing the flow velocity to decline rapidly. This would in turn force the stream to drop some of its sediment load. Depending upon a number of factors, including volume and duration of flow, a reasonably large bed of finer alluvium might accumulate. Such a deposit would provide an optimal growth environment for plants, and a small community of shrubs might become established. During subsequent flow events the plants would act to slow the flow, forcing the stream to deposit additional sediment and nutrients, building and enriching a new area of sediment for the expansion of the small plant colony. If no flow events of sufficient power to destroy the colony occurred, with the passage of time and the establishment of more plants these small communities would gradually extend themselves upstream. A self-enhancing system would be created: more and more plants slowing the stream flow more effectively, creating new sediment accumulations upstream, fostering more plant growth and new deposits for plants to colonize.

Over the course of a few hundred years these communities could have developed to the proportions seen in the visited example, eventually blocking the channel to the point that no through-flow could occur except in rare high-magnitude flow events. Given the low mean annual precipitation in this area, the probability of persistence of these riparian communities should be quite high. Only when a headcutting stream trenched a channel through them from the downstream direction, or a range fire destroyed them, would their existence be jeopardized. For prehistoric peoples, the more established of these riparian communities would have presented highly localized concentrations of leguminous trees and other plants whose pods and seeds could be gathered in season. Within the area shown in Figure 6.1, only the washes draining the older geomorphic surface show these localized riparian communities. The short, poorly integrated, multibranched drainages of this system must certainly help in the creation and maintenance of these communities.

The wash system that flows around the western side of Flatiron Mountain is a more active ephemeral stream system with a higher degree of channel integration. It is characterized by long, straight channels uninterrupted by the riparian vegetation, thus promoting through-flow. In large part, this may be due to the greater catchment area of this system to the north of the mountain, but it may also be related to the position and orientation of the mountain. The catchment area for this western part of Fourmile Wash (Figure 6.1) is roughly five times larger than that of the eastern system. Further, the channels composing it are long and relatively straight, and they flow south-southwest directly toward Flatiron Mountain. The mountain effectively terminates their flow in this direction, forcing them together into a single channel and guiding them west-southwestward around the northwestern flank of the mountain. Thus, Flatiron Mountain contributes runoff to the channel from its northern slopes.

As the stream channel passes the western end of the mountain, it emerges from a zone of confined flow in a clearly defined channel into a comparatively unconfined zone. This allows the flow to spread into a series of smaller distribution channels, decreasing both the flow depth and the flow velocity and fostering a rapid decrease in stream power. This means that the stream is much more likely to begin depositing sediment; the change is evidenced on the aerial photographs by the presence of a broad area with relatively few defined channels from the western end of the mountain until the main channel of Fourmile Wash is encountered. This broad space is the alluvial fan that has formed over a large area to the south of Flatiron Mountain and to the west of the more ancient fan surface drained by the eastern wash system. The fan surface is outlined in Figure 6.1 and is visible in Figure 1.2. Fourmile Wash is at present an entrenched stream channel that has down-cut as much as 3 m into the eastern and distal portions of the fan formed by the western drainage system.

The fan surface is composed almost exclusively of silt and silty sand with occasional linear exposures of cobble gravel that mark the positions of former channels. The dominant process on the fan over the last few thousand years has been alluviation, and examination of short backhoe trenches cut on an east-west axis across the fan revealed that the silts are at least 2.5–3.0 m thick in some places. Because no trenches were cut specifically for geologic purposes, the thickness of these fine-grained fan sediments is uncertain. The trenches also showed within the silts occasional broad, thin (10–30 cm) accumulations of pebble to small cobble gravel, marking the former locations of shallow distributary channels within the fan. Soil formation, though weak, is detectable in most parts of the fan. The backhoe trenches showed that the silt becomes increasingly clayey below 0.75–0.85 m beneath the present ground surface, suggesting the translocation of clay. There is no obvious development of soil structure. In Trench 18 at AZ T:5:12(ASM), a stage 2 carbonate horizon up to 0.60 m thick was encountered at a depth of 1.1 m below present ground surface. A roasting pit (Feature 105) lying 0.10 m above the carbonate horizon yielded a tree-ring–corrected radiocarbon date range of A.D. 860–1220. The western edge of this feature was truncated by a younger channel filled with pebble to small cobble gravels, indicating how dynamic the fan has been over the past 900 to 1,000 years in this area; there is no reason to suppose that this particular area is atypical of the fan as a whole.

Clearly this fan has been an active locus of deposition and would have been attractive to prehistoric people for its floodwater farming potential and its promotion of the growth of annual plants. These reasons are not entirely separable, but both may be important for understanding prehistoric human use of this area.

FLOODWATER FARMING

Floodwater farming was recognized in the nineteenth century as a practice common in the desert Southwest, ranging from the Colorado Plateau south to the Sonoran Desert (Clotts 1917; Cushing 1920; McGee 1898). Bryan (1929) first formally studied the use of runoff from ephemeral drainages and slopes to grow crops where direct rainfall alone might prove insufficient and where no source of permanent water for irrigation existed. He defined a class of floodwater farming that utilized alluvial fans formed at the mouth of entrenched channels as *akchin* farming, after the Tohono O'odham (formerly Papago) word for such field locations. In essence, the fields were located on various parts of the fans formed by these drainages, ranging from the apex of the fan (where the shift from confined flow within a channel to unconfined sheet or distributary flow occurred) to the distal end. Field location would be dictated by fan size, by channel position, size, length, and pattern, by topography, and by vegetation. Subsequent studies of *akchin* farming by

Hack (1942) and Nabhan (1983) have shown the wide range of variation in field location and how humans have manipulated the flow of water not only on the fans but upstream from them as well.

Waters (1987) has emphasized the dynamic nature of ephemeral stream systems. Changes brought about by deposition can lead to channel evulsion, or shifts, causing the bulk of the runoff to shift from one locus on the fan to another. These systems can also be characterized by discontinuous entrenched and unentrenched reaches within a single channel system, usually found in alternating fashion along the channel. Thus, in one area there is a headcut, below which is a reach of entrenched channel, which in turn gradually becomes shallow enough to promote the deposition of sediments and the formation of a fan. At some distance downstream of the fan is another headcut, also with its own associated entrenched channel and fan. As the headcuts proceed headward, they erode a channel into the fan of the next system upstream, finally trenching through it. The fans grow in a headward direction, however, so the whole system tends to be maintained by a balance of localized erosion and deposition. Major climatically induced shifts may favor either erosion (thus creating a single, long entrenched channel) or deposition (favoring deposition and frequent channel changes).

Traditional farmers in such settings have been shown to be keen observers of these processes and have been able to employ a variety of techniques to help minimize the undesired effects of channel changes through the use of barriers, dikes, weirs, and borders to direct and control floodwaters. Nevertheless, persistent high-frequency, low-magnitude processes and low-frequency, high-magnitude processes may eventually render a particular field location untenable, forcing relocation to another area of the fan.

It seems likely that prehistoric farmers found a situation to their liking in the fan formed by the western channel system at Flatiron Mountain. They, like their historic counterparts, probably would have located their fields in places where they could utilize runoff flowing down one of the larger distributary channels to irrigate their crops. As the positions of the channels and the areas optimal for field location changed through time, the farmers probably shifted the location of their farming efforts as well. Such adjustments may be reflected by the overall size of a site such as the Flatiron Site and the scattered activity areas it contains.

The peculiar geomorphic characteristics of this area would have provided two important advantages. First, Flatiron Mountain takes the flows of several smaller washes and concentrates them into a single stream. This gathers all the rainfall and runoff from a relatively large area, thus maximizing the potential utility of runoff from localized summer thunderstorms. The mountain thus naturally serves a function that the Tohono O'odham constructed long barriers and wing walls to achieve. Having concentrated the runoff, the western point of the mountain then acts to release the runoff from a confined channel to a shallow, unconfined channel or series of channels, encouraging deposition of sediment and dissipation of the erosive power of the stream. The accumulation of fine sediments as well as organic material creates good soil that can support plant growth. It seems that the occupants of the Flatiron Site, and perhaps other sites on or near the fan, recognized and exploited the farming potential of a rare, if not unique, set of favorable circumstances in an area that might not contain too many locations suitable for floodwater farming.

A second natural effect of an active fan is the maintenance of suitable habitat for plants that thrive in disturbed environments. This group of plants includes amaranths, chenopods, purslane, spiderling, and other taxa that are frequently found growing in recently deposited fine sediments along a channel or in areas prone to sheet flooding. These hardy annuals prefer such conditions to stable or older surfaces where perennial species usually out-compete them. These same annuals are also frequently found in agricultural fields, again loci that see disturbance in the form of cultivation and irrigation. Chenopods and amaranths (cheno-ams) in particular are frequently valued as food plants, providing both edible greens when young and abundant seeds when mature. Thus the fan, or at least portions of it, may also offer gathering opportunities where edible annual plants are concentrated. These resources, coupled with the localized riparian communities described as occurring along the channels of the washes draining the older geomorphic surface to the east of Fourmile Wash, would have provided a good source of gathered foods during the spring and particularly the summer months. The area would also have offered good floodwater farming opportunities and sufficient diversity and abundance of wild plant foods to support the people tending the fields.

ARCHAEOBOTANICAL ANALYSIS

Lisa W. Huckell

Fifteen flotation samples retrieved from three project sites were submitted for analysis. Three samples came from AZ T:5:9(ASM), one was obtained from AZ T:5:17(ASM), and eleven were collected at AZ T:5:12(ASM), the Flatiron Site. The flotation samples were almost exclusively derived from pit features that were either roasting pits or burned, shallowly excavated pits. The single exception was the sample from AZ T:5:17(ASM), which was taken from an occupation surface. The samples yielded six economic or potentially economic plant taxa and six wood taxa.

METHODS

Flotation samples were processed using the methods described by Bohrer and Adams (1977:37). After the volume was measured, each sample was passed through a fine screen into a water bath, readily visible macrofossils were removed, and all remaining dirt was added to the water. The sediment was gently agitated to free the buoyant macrofossils, and the liquid was then decanted through a 0.5 mm mesh screen. The heavy fraction was not saved.

When thoroughly dry, the samples were put through a graduated series of geological screens divided into five size classes: (1) greater than 4.75 mm, (2) between 2.0 mm and 4.75 mm, (3) between 1.0 mm and 2.0 mm, (4) between 0.495 mm and 1.0 mm, and (5) 0.495 mm or less. This strategy enhances the ease and reliability of microscopic sorting and identification, and it is useful when subsampling is required.

The analyst conducted preliminary sorting with a binocular stereo zoom microscope with a magnification range of 7–30X. Carbonization was the main criterion used to distinguish recent contaminants from those plant parts having the highest probability of affiliation with the prehistoric occupation. Unburned items were also identified and counted, and that information was used to assess the nature and degree of disturbance of sampled loci. Additional evidence of disturbance came from nonbotanical items such as small bones, fecal pellets, molluscs, and insect parts, which were also counted.

The analyst completely examined the first two size classes from each sample and often subsampled Size Classes 3 and 4 if the volume of light fraction was large. Due to time constraints and the generally poor, fragmentary condition of the material, Size Class 5 was not examined.

All complete or fragmentary items with diagnostic or distinctive features were retrieved, sorted by taxon, and placed in protective gelatin capsules. Due to time limitations, over 60 items, mainly small fragments of endosperm and other incomplete items, were not identified. Almost every analyzed sample contained unknowns.

The researcher analyzed charcoal by snapping fragments to expose fresh transverse, radial, and tangential surfaces. The specimens were examined with two incident light microscopes made available by the Laboratory of Traditional Technology, Department of Anthropology, University of Arizona. One was an Olympus DHMJ microscope with a magnification range of 50–750X, the second a Zeiss SR microscope with a magnification range of 3–98X.

Flotation charcoal from Size Classes 1, 2, and 3 was analyzed; specimens in the two remaining size classes were too small to permit efficient handling and preparation, thus considerably reducing the reliability of identifications. Each of the three size classes was subsampled, with either 15 or 25 specimens randomly selected for identification, depending on the size of the sample. When fewer than 15 fragments were present, all were identified.

Identifications of seeds and woods were made using various manuals (Parker 1972; Saul 1955) and by comparison with modern specimens in the author's collection. The taxonomy used in this study follows Kearney and Peebles (1964).

A summary of the taxa recovered from the sites is presented in Table 7.1.

Table 7.1. Plant Taxa Recovered from the Fourmile Wash Sites

Scientific Name	Common Name
Gramineae sp.	
Zea mays L.	corn, maize
Chenopodiaceae sp.	
Atriplex cf. *canescens* (Pursh) Nutt	four-wing saltbush, cenizo
Amaranthaceae sp.	
Cactaceae	
Opuntia sp.	prickly pear, beavertail cactus
Nyctaginaceae	
Boerhaavia cf. *coccinea* Mill	spiderling
Malvaceae	
Sphaeralcea sp.	globe mallow
Leguminosae	
Prosopis juliflora (Swartz) DC var. velutina (Woot.) Sarg	velvet mesquite
Cercidium microphyllum (Torr.) Rose & Johnston	littleleaf palo verde
Cercidium floridum Benth.	blue palo verde
Olneya tesota Gray	ironwood
Zygophyllaceae	
Larrea tridentata (DC) Coville	creosote bush

RESULTS

Results of the analysis indicated that some disturbance of feature deposits had occurred. Varying quantities of insect exoskeletal fragments (particularly those of ants and beetles), fecal pellets, snails, rootlets, and small vertebrate bones and teeth were present. Modern seeds and plant parts (anthers, capsule fragments, leaves, and leaflets) also were found, including seeds of *Plantago* (plantain), *Euphorbia* (spurge), *Erodium* (filaree), *Kallstroemia*, *Echinocereus* (hedgehog cactus), Chenopodiaceae and Amaranthaceae (cheno-ams), Gramineae (grasses), Malvaceae (mallow family), Cruciferae (mustard family), and Boraginaceae (borage family). All specimens were carbonized.

The analysis results are given in Table 7.2. In the entries in the table consisting of a pair of figures, the upper figure presents the actual numbers of the item counted, while the parenthetical figure immediately below represents an estimate of the total number of items present in the complete sample. Dual columns are also provided for *Zea* (maize) cupules and cheno-ams. The first column gives the number of complete or nearly complete (greater than one-half) items, while the second lists the number of fragments for which less than one-half of the item was present. This approach enables the counts to be more effectively evaluated in terms of the actual quantity of a taxon present.

Zea mays

Maize remains were recovered from AZ T:5:12(ASM), the Flatiron Site. These consisted of 41 cupules and cupule fragments, 2 probable kernel fragments, and 2 glumes (Table 7.2). Most of the cupules were too fragmentary for measurements to be taken. Those that were relatively intact (n=5) yielded widths between 3.2 mm and 7.1 mm, with an average width of 4.41 mm. These figures must be accepted cautiously as minimum width indications, since all of the specimens had sustained some degree of damage to the rachis flaps or cupule wings, making it impossible to obtain an accurate predamage dimension. The only cupule suitable for a height measurement yielded a figure of 2.8 mm. Cupule shapes varied considerably, ranging from square to trapezoidal to a broad, strongly compressed rectangle.

Two badly damaged fragments of what appeared to be kernels were also recovered. They seemed to be portions of the rounded, smooth, apical cap area of the kernel. Two fragmentary lower glumes, the chaffy bracts that enclose the kernel, were also found. Neither was complete enough for measurement.

Maize has been the staff of life for many Southwestern cultures. It comes in a wide variety of colors and several kernel textures, which often dictate how the corn is prepared. For insight into the importance of maize as well as the myriad ways in which it is prepared, see Cushing (1920), Whiting (1939), and Castetter and Bell (1942).

Cheno-ams

Cheno-ams include members of the Chenopodiaceae and Amaranthaceae. This term is generally applied to weedy, usually herbaceous species that are an important source of copious quantities of small, very nutritious seeds and edible greens (Gasser 1982:221–22) and are available from early spring to late fall. Their consistent and often abundant presence in the archaeobotanical record (Gasser 1982:Table 1; Huckell 1986:Table 12.4) suggests that they were a valued food resource for the Hohokam. Their small size and the common preparation technique of parching the seeds

Table 7.2. Plant Macrofossils Recovered from the Fourmile Wash Sites

Site (ASM)	FN	Vol. (ML)	Fest. No.	Fest. Type	ZCF >%	ZCF <%	CFZ	ZG	CA >%	CA <%	OS	BF	MS	SPH	GC	GCF	LS	Unk	Total
AZ T:5:9	19	5250	9	rp															●
	21	4900	9	rp															●
	22	1800	8	rp															●
AZ T:5:12	93	4600	3	rp		5			27	10						3		2	45
	102	6200	45	bp		9			4							1		(6)	17
	111	5800	107	bp		9			(18)									3	(35)
	113	3250	100	bp	1	5		1										(5)	9 (11)
	128	6900	103	rp	21 (30)	5	2	1	1 (4)									6	33 (39)
	130	4400	103	rp			2	1	353 (701)	84 (159)			1 (2)			1		10 (18)	449 (881)
	133	7500	105	rp					12 (144)	12 (144)						1		3 (16)	28 (305)
	134	7450	111	rp					16 (99)	32 (205)	1			1				4 (26)	52 (339)
	154	2350	113	rp					13	1	1				1	2	9	7	15
	155	5500	113	rp	2	2										2	(11)	(15)	20 (34)
	353	4200	28	rp	2				5 (20)							+		8	13 (51)
AZ T:5:17	39	6050	5	oa					15 (38)			1	3 (8)	3	1	1		7	31 (59)

FN - Field Number
Vol - Volume
Fest - Feature

ZCF - Zea cupule fragments
CFZ - cf. Zea kernel fragments
ZG - Zea glumes
CA - Cheno-ams

OS - *Opuntia* seed
BF - *Boerhavia* fruit
MS - Malvaceae seeds
SPH - *Sphaeralcea*

GC - Gramineae caryopses
GCM - Gramineae culm fragments
LS - Legume spines
Unk - Unknown

oa - occupation surface
bp - burned pit
rp - roasting pit
+More than 1000 specimens in sample, not counted

PARENTHETICAL FIGURES: All numbers enclosed in parentheses (98) are estimated numbers of that item in the sample. Because some samples were subsampled, the actual total number is unknown and had to be estimated. The regular numbers indicate the actual number of a given taxon that was recovered.

prior to grinding them into flour or meal substantially increased the chances of spillage into the cooking fire, where carbonization could take place.

Cheno-am seeds were recovered from AZ T:5:17(ASM) and AZ T:5:12(ASM) (Table 7.2). The specimens from the first site were all badly broken, very likely the unfortunate result of this sample having been subjected to the flotation process a second time.

Those from AZ T:5:12(ASM), the Flatiron Site, were in better condition. Based on those specimens still retaining some diagnostic features, the assemblage appeared to consist almost entirely of chenopod-like seeds, the major possible exception being the fragmentary seeds from Feature 28, which more closely resembled amaranths.

Measurements for some of the chenopod seeds were possible. Seed diameters (n=21) ranged between 0.6 mm and 0.95 mm, with a mean of 0.78 mm. Thicknesses (n=10) fell between 0.3 mm and 0.5 mm, with a mean of 0.42 mm.

Opuntia

A single seed of a prickly pear was recovered from Feature 103, a roasting pit at AZ T:5:12(ASM). The intact seed with its conspicuous, well-developed marginal rim measured 2.6 mm in height, 2.9 mm in width, and 1.6 mm in thickness.

Prickly pear fruits have been widely used for food by many Southwestern ethnic groups. The large, sweet, juicy fruits become available during the hot summer months, providing welcome, often abundant food that is usually eaten raw after the removal of the tiny spines, or glochids. The fruits also may be cooked into syrup and jam (Castetter and Bell 1942:60; Castetter and Underhill 1935:46; Curtin 1984:61). The seeds have not generally been used for food, although at least one group, the Cahuilla of southern California, made mush from the ground seeds of *O. basilaris* (Bean and Saubel 1972:95).

Prickly pear seeds occasionally are recovered from Hohokam sites, but invariably in very small quantities (Gasser 1982:Table 1; Huckell 1986:Table 12.4). This modest presence may be largely attributable to the consumption of the fruit in its raw state, which removes it from the vicinity of the cooking fire, or to the cooking of the fruits by boiling, which again limits the opportunities for exposure to the carbonizing fire. This latter preparation method probably also ensured the discard of seeds as residue at the nonvillage processing area or on the local trash dump, where decay and animal predation would have rapidly removed them from the archaeobotanical record.

Sphaeralcea

Four seeds assignable to the genus *Sphaeralcea* of the Malvaceae, or mallow family, were recovered from two sites: three from the use surface at AZ T:5:17(ASM) and one from Feature 103, a pit at AZ T:5:12(ASM). The smooth, apostrophe-shaped seeds averaged 0.9 mm in height, 1.0 mm in width, and 0.5 mm in thickness. The genus includes a number of showy, common desert perennial herbs that tend to prefer disturbed soils.

Apart from cotton, members of this family appear to have played an insignificant role in Southwestern aboriginal economies. However, *Sphaeralcea* species appear to have enjoyed widespread use as medicinal and ceremonial plants (Curtin 1984:80–81; Elmore 1944:63; Robbins et al. 1916:60–61; Russell 1975:79; Stevenson 1915:98; Vestal 1952:36). The Navajo chewed the roots of *S. coccinea* (Pursh.) Rydb. during food shortages and also may have eaten the seeds of *S. lobata* Wooton (Elmore 1944:63). Small quantities of the seeds of this genus have been recovered from Hohokam sites (Gasser 1982:Table 1), where they may represent an undocumented use for food, the stored raw materials for medicinal preparations, or the inadvertent introduction of the seeds into feature contexts through unrelated activities.

Boerhaavia

A single fruit, probably of *Boerhaavia* cf. *coccinea*, was recovered from Feature 5, the occupation surface at AZ T:5:17(ASM). The elongated, ovate fruit was somewhat distorted from the heat, but it still bore five distinct longitudinal ridges. It measured 2.0 mm in height and 0.9 mm at its maximum diameter.

The genus *Boerhaavia* (spiderling) includes a number of weedy species that colonize and thrive on disturbed soils such as those of yards, pathways, and agricultural fields. Ethnographic accounts suggest that the plants were seldom utilized by Southwestern groups. Among the Seri of coastal northern Sonora, however, the herbage of *B. coulteri* (Hook.f.) S.Wats. was cooked, mashed, and eaten (Felger and Moser 1985:349). The Tepehuan of Chihuahua made a tea from the leaves of *B. mirabilis* that was drunk for fever (Ford 1975:301).

Gramineae

Grass remains, including culm (stem) fragments and a single caryopsis (grain), were recovered. Grass stem fragments were found only in small numbers in several of the pit features, although Feature 28 at AZ T:5:12(ASM) contained over 1,000 fragments (Table 7.2). The culms were all less than 2.0 mm in diameter and contained a solid pith. The grass grain came from the occupation surface at AZ T:5:17(ASM). It was long, slender, and cylindrical, with a length of 6.0 mm and a diameter of 1.3 mm.

Many species of grasses, both wild and domesticated, have provided food to Southwestern peoples (Doebley 1984). The stems, leaves, and pollen have made valuable economic contributions in the form of arrow shafts, pads, brushes, thatching, food wrappers, ceremonial materials, as a source of sugar, and more. They also have made convenient buffer materials in roasting pits, protecting the cooking food from being scorched or damaged by contact with the hot coals.

Wood Charcoal

Wood charcoal was obtained from all three sites investigated, with all of the specimens coming from flotation samples. Six genera were represented in the 645 fragments analyzed (Table 7.3). The results indicated that *Prosopis* (mesquite) had been the overwhelming choice for fuel wood. Mesquite accounted for 152 (92%) of the identifiable fragments at AZ T:5:9(ASM) and represented 267 (57%) of the total at AZ T:5:12(ASM). Mesquite was not present in the single sample analyzed from AZ T:5:17(ASM). Of the remaining wood species, *Atriplex* (saltbush), *Cercidium microphyllum* (littleleaf palo verde), *C. floridum* (blue palo verde), *Olneya* (ironwood), and *Larrea* (creosote bush) each accounted for less than 7% of the total, with the exception of the very small, single sample from AZ T:5:17(ASM), which was composed almost entirely of saltbush and ironwood.

Table 7.3. Wood Charcoal Recovered from the Fourmile Wash Sites

Site (ASM)	Field Number	Feature Number	PRO	LAR	ATR	OLN	CF	CM	CCM	CS	GC	UNI	Total
AZ T:5:9	19	9	64		3			3				5	75
	21	9	64									1	65
	22	8	24									1	25
AZ T:5:12	93	3	19		1	4	1					2	22
	102	45	7			1		2				8	22
	111	107	28		6	1	5					6	46
	113	100	1				1		9			6	17
	128	103	45	4		4	1					6	60
	130	103	4	2	24	1		3				1	38
	133	105	31	3		2	7	9				7	60
	134	111	43	2		1		13		1		1	60
	154	113	20			1		1				8	35
	155	113	36									14	50
	353	28	33	5		1	10					8	60
AZ T:5:17	39	5			4	8					3	3	15

PRO – *Prosopis*
LAR – *Larrea*
ATR – *Atriplex*
OLN – *Olneya*

CF – *Cercidium floridum*
CM – *Cercidium microphyllum*
CCM – *Cercidium cf. microphyllum*

CS – *Cercidium sp.*
GC – Gramineae culms
UNI – Unidentified

The extremely low percentages of nonmesquite genera in the wood charcoal assemblage probably reflected foraging for dead and down or easily broken up woods to augment the mesquite fuel supply, or they may have been woods that were simply close by or convenient to collect. All of the species are present in the study area today.

DISCUSSION

Several analytical concepts have been devised that aid in the assessment of the relative importance of archaeobotanical taxa recovered. They include presence value, parts per liter, and relative abundance based on percent of total.

Presence value is the proportion of the total number of flotation samples that contain a taxon (Hubbard 1980:52). It has been used to provide some measure of the taxon's importance, as it is assumed that the greater the number of samples in which it appears, the greater the importance of that taxon. This measure allows some degree of quantitative comparison, something that is difficult to do with simple counts because of the lack of accurate knowledge concerning what those counts really represent (Hubbard 1980:51).

Parts per liter is a seed-volume index that is calculated by dividing the total number of a taxon by the total number of liters examined that contained usable taxa (Gasser 1987:303). This index has been employed to compare taxon variability between features, feature classes, and sites (Gasser 1987, 1988). Based on his extensive work with Hohokam archaeobotanical remains, Gasser (1987:303) has found that this value is usually less than 1.00 parts per liter (ppl). Higher values, particularly those exceeding 5.00 ppl, are significant and may be indicative of feature function or site specialization.

The relative abundance of a taxon, based on its percentage of the total, is a simple percentage derived by dividing the total number of a taxon by the total number of items recovered. This statistic simply indicates the portion of the total macroplant assemblage taken by each taxon. This is another relative measure of use, as higher percentages again suggest greater use. Barring sampling bias, these statistics should present complementary results.

The two major objectives of this study were (1) to apply the macrofossil evidence recovered toward identifying the subsistence base of the inhabitants of the study area and (2) to see if feature contents could suggest feature function.

Of the sites providing samples for flotation analysis, AZ T:5:9(ASM) produced no economic remains and was therefore not subject to statistical consideration. AZ T:5:17(ASM) yielded a single sample from one feature, a data set too limited to be of real significance for the purposes of site comparison. Results were much better at AZ T:5:12(ASM), where 10 flotation samples from 8 pits yielded economically significant taxa (Table 7.4). Researchers used estimated counts to construct the table, giving all fragments equal weight with the more complete specimens. The liter total includes only those samples containing macrofossils.

SUBSISTENCE

As indicated in Table 7.2, the macrofloral record from AZ T:5:12(ASM) was completely dominated by two taxa, maize and cheno-ams. Maize accounted for 3.5% of the total estimated number of identified economic plant parts, while cheno-ams constituted an overwhelming 96% of

Table 7.4. Summary of Carbonized Economic Taxa from AZ T:5:12(ASM), Fourmile Wash
Project

Taxon	Estimated Taxon Total	Number of Samples with Taxon	Presence Value (%)	Parts per Liter	Relative Abundance (% of Total)
Zea	56	5	50	1.05	3.5
Cheno-ams	1545	8	80	28.85	96.0
Sphaeralcea	2	1	10	0.04	0.0
Opuntia	1	1	10	0.02	0.0

Total number samples = 10; estimated total number of carbonized items = 1604; total liters analyzed = 53.55.
Presence Value = Number of samples with taxon divided by total number of flotation samples.
Parts per Liter = Estimated taxon total divided by total liters containing economic taxa.
Relative Abundance (% of Total) = Estimated taxon total divided by total number of carbonized items.

the total. Presence values and the number of parts per liter also demonstrated the dominance of these two taxa. *Sphaeralcea* and *Opuntia* were present in such small quantities as to be insignificant. Figures for Feature 5, the use surface at AZ T:5:17(ASM) (Table 7.2), showed a similar though not quite as impressive presence of maize and cheno-ams. Here again, minimal appearances were made by three other taxa.

With the absence of corroborative or supplemental information from the pollen analysis carried out for study area sites (Chapter 8), these data constituted the best available information on site subsistence. The picture they created is one of virtual total reliance on cheno-ams and maize by local inhabitants. The surprising lack of species diversity in the taxonomic inventory may have been a problem of sampling error, but it also suggested that commonly exploited, locally available wild plant foods such as mesquite and palo verde beans may not have been available during the season when the sites were occupied, or that dietary diversity was sublimated to the task of growing a limited, very specific crop inventory. The absence of domestic features such as houses or hearths from the sampled portions of the sites precluded comparison with macrofossil assemblages generated by small-scale, domestic consumption that could contain either a more varied inventory reflecting idiosyncratic supplementary wild plant usage or the nearly exclusive reliance on cheno-ams and maize that would be consistent with the concept of crop specialization. Whether the cheno-ams were crop plants or wild species that were encouraged as field weeds is open to question, as domesticated forms of *Amaranthus* and possibly *Chenopodium* have been identified at Hohokam sites (Gasser 1988:226, 228). The evidence offered by the remaining taxa was equivocal. Most were weedy species that could easily have been contaminants. The available ethnographic literature on preparation methods for these plants does not include pit baking or roasting, which again suggests that the specimens could have been trash. The widespread occurrence of small amounts of globe mallow at Hohokam sites (Gasser 1988:Table 70, Table 80; Miksicek 1984:Table 11.2.4) hints at its deliberate exploitation, but for what use is currently unknown.

FUNCTIONAL ANALYSIS

Three morphologically distinct features were sampled for macrofossil remains: roasting pits consisting of aggregations of fire-cracked rocks in or adjacent to excavated basins of various sizes; burned pits composed of ash- and charcoal-filled depressions; and a use surface, a compacted tan-brown layer forming a surface punctuated by pits and depressions (Chapter 4), which contained all three of the burned pits. Researchers evaluated the flotation results to attempt to discover whether the two distinct pit types served similar or different functions. All of the roasting pits and two of the burned pits contained cheno-ams. Evaluation of the macrofossil contents of the two pit types (Table 7.2) indicated that the roasting pits were dominated by the presence of cheno-ams, at 38.36 ppl. Cheno-ams were found in the burned pits in considerably smaller quantity, 3.61 ppl, a number that is still well above the usual for Hohokam plant taxa. The high values supported the interpretation that the roasting pits, and very probably the burned pits as well, had been utilized for the preparation of cheno-ams. The potentially skewing effect of the exceptionally high estimated contents of three roasting pits, Features 103, 105, and 111 (Table 7.2), was offset by the 2.82 ppl value obtained for the remaining roasting pits and the near ubiquity of the seeds, which appeared in seven of the eight (87.5%) features from AZ T:5:12(ASM) that were sampled.

As mentioned earlier, the most widespread method of preparing cheno-am seeds was to parch them with or over hot coals prior to their being ground into flour, an approach that did not require a pit. The Mojave, Yuma, Maricopa, and Cocopa subjected seeds of the chenopod species *Atriplex lentiformis* (Torr.) S. Wats., a saltbush, to pit baking as a part of the preparation process (Castetter and Bell 1951:188–89; Spier 1970:52–53). The fruits were gathered in November or December and pounded and winnowed several times to free the seeds from the tough, enclosing bracts. The rest of the procedure is described by Castetter and Bell (1951:188–89): "First a pit was dug and the bottom lined with stones. These were thoroughly heated by building a fire on them; after the ashes were removed a quantity of soaked seeds was piled in the pit, covered with a layer of moist earth and thus baked, aided by a fire kept burning on top of the pit for several hours." The seeds were then parched and ground.

No mention is made of the use of a protective, confining layer of greens placed around the seeds, in which case there would be ample opportunity for some of the tiny seeds to be left in the pit. The Pima employed the same process for the same species, the only difference being that the seeds were enclosed in a wrapper of *Suaeda*, or seep weed (another chenopod genus), and cottonwood bark (Russell 1975:78). Although this preparation method appears to be restricted to saltbush, it is possible that the Hohokam could have adopted it for use on locally available cheno-am species. Tentative evidence for the use of a protective grass layer came from Feature 28, an eroded roasting pit containing a very large concentration of grass stems (Table 7.2). Cheno-am seeds could also have been introduced into the pits as passengers on mature greenery such as *Suaeda* that was used to form the protective layer in the pits. Saltbush was often used to flavor roasting foods and could also have served in that capacity as a vector to introduce seeds into pits.

The maize remains were somewhat less convincing indicators of pit function. Maize was present in all three burned pits (1.38 ppl) and two of the five roasting pits (0.91 ppl) (Table 7.2). Maize ears were often roasted to alter the flavor, improve grinding quality, and enhance storage capability. The Hopi (Beaglehole 1937:67) and the Zuni (Cushing 1920:204–8) used huge roasting pits able to hold many dozens of ears. The Pima and Tohono O'odham (formerly the Papago) used two methods. The first involved firing piles of unhusked ears covered with brush for several minutes until they were partially roasted. The second involved roasting the ears on coals made in open pits of unspecified size (Castetter and Bell 1942:181–82).

It is certainly possible that the maize remains from the Fourmile Wash features were remnants of pit-roasted ears. Two probable kernel fragments found in Feature 103 could have been lost during the roasting process. It is equally possible that the material was trash containing fragments of burned corn cobs used for fuel. A case in point is Feature 113, a roasting pit and associated deposit of material that had been removed from the feature prehistorically. Field Number (FN) 154 was taken from the cleaned-out material, and FN 155 was taken from the pit fill (Table 7.2). The cleaned-out material contained cheno-ams and no maize, whereas the fill contained maize and no cheno-ams. The fill containing the two maize cupule fragments consisted of alluvial deposits along with ash pockets and charcoal. This evidence suggested that the pit had been used in cheno-am processing and then gradually filled with trash and silts after its abandonment. Such contamination probably occurred readily due to the generation of large quantities of charred debris on the site surface by the roasting or surface-cooking processes, trash that could easily have been redeposited by eolian or alluvial means into open, exposed pits and depressions.

Another factor that should be considered here is the possible reuse of pits, often for the preparation of different foodstuffs (Greenhouse et al. 1981:232). Depending on the degree to which the pit had been cleaned following each use, an accumulation of successive use residues could have developed or been churned together, obscuring evidence belying what is often assumed to be a single function for the pit. Such a situation could also account for the mixed maize–cheno-am assemblages obtained from four of the pits (Table 7.2).

It should be noted that four of the roasting pits sampled contained no economic plant remains (Table 7.2). This could have been the result of erosion, of preservation biases, or of the use of the pits for preparation of meat.

Little can be said regarding the use surface from AZ T:5:17(ASM). The 6.30 ppl value for cheno-ams suggested that occupants of this site had relied substantially on them. However, the feature was discovered at a depth of just 5 cm below the modern ground surface and had exceptionally large numbers of modern seeds, fecal pellets, and insect parts in the flotation residue. This suggested that the feature had been significantly affected by bioturbation, a process that could also have accounted for the presence of the three carbonized weedy taxa (Table 7.2) and possibly the cheno-ams as well, given their presence in an unconfined open context.

CONCLUSIONS

The sites in the Fourmile Wash Project area appeared to reflect opportunistic behavior on the part of the site occupants, who had recognized the agricultural potential of the unique geomorphological setting around and to the south of Flatiron Mountain. As B. Huckell (Chapter 6) suggests, floodwater farming was probably carried out at many places on the alluvial fan deposits, with maize and cheno-ams the primary crops cultivated or harvested. The duration of site occupation could have been as brief as three months, particularly if the farmers were growing strains of maize that matured quickly and had low water needs, such as Papago 60-Day corn (Castetter and Bell 1942:81–82), which could have been available three months after the arrival of the summer rains allowed planting to begin. This would place the time of the occupation between late June or early July and September or early October. The crops could then have been harvested, processed at the growing sites, and transported back to more permanent residential locations where the food could be stored or distributed. The bulk of the archaeological data indicated that extensive processing of plant materials had taken place at area sites with numerous thermal features. Of these, two major pit types, the rock-filled roasting pit and the burned, ash-filled pit, were sampled. The results indicated that there was no clear-cut functional distinction between the two types, as both contained cheno-ams and maize in quantities that indicated both foods could have been prepared in them.

Did the occupants of AZ T:5:17(ASM) and AZ T:5:12(ASM) subsist essentially entirely on maize and cheno-ams? The macrobotanical evidence says yes, but there is no way to be certain. In addition to sampling bias, preservational bias is a major problem, for soft foods such as greens, tubers, and seed flours would not have endured in the record. Eating plant parts raw or using preparation methods such as boiling would have ensured that no remains would be preserved. Preservation is thus heavily biased toward durable items such as maize cobs, nut shells, hard seeds, and so forth, giving researchers a somewhat lopsided dietary picture at best.

However monotonous it may have been, a diet of maize and cheno-ams (with perhaps some added meat from rabbits or birds) may have offered some advantages in the form of enhanced nutrition. Some amaranth seeds contain high levels of critical amino acids that occur at low levels in maize, while maize contains high levels of some amino acids found at low levels in amaranths (National Research Council 1984:34–35). When the two plant types are combined in the diet, they yield an amino acid level approaching the optimum protein balance needed by human beings. In addition, both amaranth and chenopod greens are good sources of vitamin A and calcium (Meals For Millions/Freedom from Hunger Foundation 1980:21) and can be harvested from the plants without affecting future seed yields.

PALYNOLOGICAL ANALYSIS

Suzanne K. Fish

Researchers analyzed five pollen samples from three sites: AZ T:5:11(ASM), AZ T:5:12(ASM), and AZ T:5:17(ASM). Sampled contexts included occupation surfaces, rock piles, and pits. Environmental and economic patterns at all three sites exhibited limited evidence for disturbance and resource use (Table 8.1).

METHODS

Extraction was performed in the Department of Geosciences, University of Arizona. Researchers deflocculated 60 cc of each sample with dilute hydrochloric acid, then added *Lycopodium* spore tracers to the solution to permit evaluation of the extraction procedure. A swirl and timed settling rate as described by Mehringer (1967:136–37) was employed to initially separate the lighter pollen-bearing fraction from other soil materials. Heavy liquid flotation with zinc bromide of 2.0 density further reduced the sample matrix. Residual silicates were removed with hydrofluoric acid.

After mounting the extract in glycerol, researchers viewed each sample at a magnification of 600X and identified a standard sum of 200 pollen grains, which has been shown to adequately register representative distributions of common pollen types from Southwestern vegetation (Martin 1963:30–31). The standard sum is the basis for percentage calculations of the types presented in Table 8.1. After tabulation was completed, additional material was scanned at lower magnification to detect rare types. Identifications made only in scanning are indicated in the table. Types occurring in aggregates of six or more grains also are noted. Since clusters would be less efficiently transported by wind than single grains, aggregates may indicate a locationally immediate source for the pollen. A more detailed discussion of procedures can be found in Fish 1984.

RESULTS

Pollen spectra from all three sites were generally similar in distribution of major types reflecting site environment. At each site, the dominant pollen was *Ambrosia*-type, contributed by bursage. This is typically the case for creosote-bursage associations, including ones in which desert arboreals are important components (Hevly et al. 1965; Schoenwetter and Doerschlag 1971). Trace amounts of mesquite (*Prosopis*) and palo verde (*Cercidium*) were also encountered, representing local tree forms.

Sunflower family (Compositae) pollen with high spines was relatively more abundant at AZ T:5:11(ASM). Since elevated quantities were present in both site samples, it is probable that vegetational rather than cultural patterns are reflected. The plant habitat may have been somewhat more mesic, although other local edaphic factors could also be involved.

Pollen of weedy species, encouraged by cultural disturbance, occurred in low quantities at all three sites. The extent and intensity of occupational alteration of site environment appeared to have been limited. Pollen of chenopods and amaranths (cheno-ams) was elevated at a single site.

Table 8.1. Frequencies of Pollen Types in Samples

Site (ASM)	Pollen Type																		
	AMB	ART	HSC	CHE	GRA	BOE	SPH	KAL	ONA	ERI	EUP	GIL	PRO	CER	LEG	EPH	PIN	QUE	IND
AZ T:5:17																			
Feature 5	64.0		10.5	4.0	3.0	2.5	9.0*	+		+		0.5		+	1.0	2.0	1.0		2.5
AZ T:5:11																			
Feature 1	52.5		20.5	6.0	7.5	4.0	5.0								0.5	1.5	0.5		2.0
Feature 12	45.0		27.0	7.5	6.0	4.0	+		0.5						1.0	2.5	3.5		3.0
AZ T:5:12																			
Feature 103	40.5	+	10.0	36.0*	2.5	2.5	3.0*			1.5	0.5				2.0	1.0	+	+	0.5
Feature 109	48.0		15.5	21.0*	4.0	1.5	+			2.0	1.5		1.0			1.5	1.0		3.0

AMB - *Ambrosia*-type   CHE - Cheno-am   GIL - *Gilia*   KAL - *Kallstroemia*   PRO - *Prosopis*
ART - *Artemisia*   EPH - *Ephedra*   GRA - Gramineae   LEG - Leguminosae   QUE - *Quercus*
BOE - *Boerhaavia*-type   ERI - *Eriogonum*   HSC - High-Spine Compositae   ONA - Onagraceae   SPH - *Sphaeralcea*
CER - *Cercidium*   EUP - *Euphorbia*-type   IND - Indeterminate   PIN - *Pinus*

* Indicates a pollen type occuring in aggregates of six or more grains.
+ Indicates a pollen type encountered only in scanning after completion of the 200-grain standard sum.

In this case, cultural introduction is probable.   Types commonly associated with Hohokam agricultural contexts (Fish 1985) also were encountered in low quantities.   Spiderling (*Boerhaavia*), usually the most abundant of these types, was always less than 5%.   Globe mallow (*Sphaeralcea*) values were higher than those of spiderling, and this species was probably most numerous in site environs.   Cultural introduction may again have been responsible for higher percentages and aggregates.

AZ T:5:11(ASM)

Two samples from rock piles at AZ T:5:11(ASM) provided only negative evidence for resource use or cultural activity.   Parallel distributions of types in the two samples failed to reveal any evidence of cultural bias through the introduction of plant materials, nor was there any indication of environmental disturbance consistent with cultivation of adjacent fields or even extended occupation.

AZ T:5:12(ASM), the Flatiron Site

Two samples — one from beneath a metate in Feature 103 (a pit) and one from beneath a rock on the surface of Occupation Surface 2 — yielded higher percentages of cheno-am pollen, suggesting resource use, in comparison with the substantially lower percentages at the other sites.   These elevated amounts could also have been produced by vegetation in the site vicinity.   Greater densities of species such as saltbush (*Atriplex*) or weedy herbaceous plants flourishing in culturally disturbed habitats could have been responsible.   Differing percentages between the two samples appeared to reflect the locational bias of differentially introduced plant materials. The presence of aggregates in both cases strengthened this inference.

Few chenopods and amaranths are gathered in the earlier spring months.   If the aggregates of globe mallow in the pit are indicative of a resource, utilized plants at the site would be commensurate with summer gathering, although globe mallow tends to bloom more opportunistically with available moisture.

AZ T:5:17(ASM)

The single sample was collected beneath a mano on the occupation surface, Feature 5.   Globe mallow pollen occurred in aggregates and in the highest percentage among samples from all sites. Although a resource use was probably indicated, a direct association with the mano is problematical. The most widespread ethnographic use recorded for globe mallow in southern Arizona is as a medicinal plant (Curtin 1984; Russell 1975).   The Navajo ate the seeds (Elmore 1944), and the Hopi chewed the stems (Castetter 1935); it is possible that prehistoric groups gathered globe mallow upon occasion as well, particularly where the plants were abundant.

FAUNAL ANALYSIS

Linda J. Pierce

The Fourmile Wash excavations produced a small collection of mammalian faunal remains from two sites. A total of 65 bones and bone fragments were recovered from AZ T:5:12(ASM), and 119 bone fragments were found at AZ T:5:17(ASM).

Investigators cleaned all animal bone from these excavations with toothbrush and dental pick and identified the specimens using the WAC comparative collection housed in the Arizona State Museum. Due to the fragmentary nature of the bone, most taxonomic identifications could only be made securely to class or order level.

As much as possible of the following information was recorded for each bone or bone fragment: taxonomic classification, element, side (if applicable), and portion of bone (proximal, distal end, etc.). In addition, any indication of burning or other cultural modification was noted. If the bone was only a fragment, researchers estimated the percentage of the total element that was present. In cases where a bone fragment could only be identified to a class level (mammal), the size of the animal was estimated.

The faunal collection from AZ T:5:12(ASM), the Flatiron Site, was very small. Still, a few observations regarding the assemblage could be made. First, the 14 bones identified as being from a kangaroo rat (*Dipodomys* cf. *deserti*) were from a single skeleton and represented an intrusive burrow death. Only one bone in the collection was from a jackrabbit (*Lepus*). The majority of the bone in the assemblage represented large mammals, either deer or antelope (Artiodactyla). Many of these bones were very fragmented, and 65% were burned, indicating human exploitation. In addition, one rib fragment with cut marks was tentatively identified as having come from a mule deer (*Odocoileus hemionus*).

Although the faunal assemblage (n=119) from AZ T:5:17(ASM) was larger than that from AZ T:5:12(ASM), it represented fewer animals. The vast majority (n=115) were fragments from large mammals, probably representing a maximum of five bones. The fragments were very small slivers, which appeared to be the result of bone erosion and decomposition. A few of the slivers were burned, again indicating cultural use. Given the very fragmented nature of the large mammal bones, the collection from this site was actually very small, and it is difficult to make any more specific remarks regarding it.

FAUNAL DESCRIPTIONS

AZ T:5:12 (ASM), the Flatiron Site

Feature 45, a pit in an occupation surface (Feature 106), yielded a variety of faunal remains. Only one fragment was found at Feature 45, FN 108: an *Odocoileus hemionus* (mule deer) right ulna. This bone, a burned shaft, articulated with the ulna fragment from FN 109.

Another *O. hemionus* fragment, also part of a burned right ulna shaft, was found at Feature 45, FN 109. This fragment fit with the ulna fragment from FN 108 and possibly with the one from FN 110. A distal condyle fragment from the first or second phalange of an Artiodactyla was also found at this site. Fifteen long-bone shaft fragments, probably of deer or antelope, were recovered. Seven of them were burned.

Feature 45, FN 110, contained a right ulna, proximal end, fused and burned, from an *O. hemionus*. A burned long-bone shaft fragment from a small mammal (probably rabbit) was also found.

Feature 45, FN 208, contained several fragments: a right burned scapula fragment from a glenoid fossa; a burned right squamosal (skull fragment); a right innominate ischium fragment, unfused, from an immature *Lepus californicus* (black-tailed jackrabbit); and a burned dorsal spine from an *O. hemionus* thoracic vertebra. Also found were two pieces of one vertebra centrum, unfused and slightly burned; a lumbar vertebra fragment, burned; a dorsal spine from a thoracic vertebra; and a burned rib shaft, all from Artiodactyla cf. *O. hemionus*. Although broken, burned, and rodent-gnawed, the fragments were mostly reconstructible. The rib shaft had numerous small, thin crosswise cuts around it. Another Artiodactyla rib shaft fragment was also recovered, as were two long-bone shaft fragments, both burned, from a medium or large mammal (larger than rabbit), and five unidentified bone fragments, three of them burned.

Feature 45, FN 212, contained an Artiodactyla cf. *O. hemionus* lumbar vertebra fragment and an Artiodactyla right scapula fragment, both burned. Seven small long-bone shaft fragments from a large mammal were also found; four of them were burned.

FN 327 from Feature 103, a pit in an occupation surface (Feature 109), contained a left femur shaft fragment from *L. californicus*. Two long-bone shaft fragments, probably from the femur, were also found.

A partial skeleton of a *Dipodomys* cf. *deserti* (the large size suggested desert kangaroo rat) found in Feature 105 (a roasting pit), FN 136, included the skull, right mandible, sacrum, right and left innominate, right and left tibia, left femur, right and left ulna, right radius, right ulna, and two metatarsals. Most likely the animal was intrusive into the site.

Feature 105, FN 369, included an intrusive den death of a *D. deserti*.

FN 121 from Feature 107, a pit in an occupation surface (Feature 106), included a fragment of of a proximal metapodial from an Artiodactyla. Two burned fragments of a large mammal long-bone shaft, probably pieces of one badly eroded bone, were also found.

Feature 113, a burned pit and occupation surface, FN 151, contained a right innominate fragment from the ilium of a *L. californicus* and one long-bone shaft fragment, also probably from a jackrabbit.

AZ T:5:17(ASM)

All the faunal remains from this site were recovered from Feature 5, an occupation surface. FN 22 contained 5 fragments of long-bone shaft from a large mammal (probably Artiodactyla); three were slightly burned.

FN 23 included the shaft of the left femur from a *Neotoma* sp. (wood rat). The feature also included five fragments of a long-bone shaft from a large mammal (probably Artiodactyla). The fragments were probably the remains of one bone. Other large mammal (probably Artiodactyla) remains included 15 fragments of a long-bone shaft, possibly the remains of one very fractured and eroded bone. Another group of large mammal (probably Artiodactyla) remains included 28 very small long-bone shaft fragments, probably the eroded remnants of one bone. The proximal end of an Artiodactyla metapodial was also found.

FN 29 contained five fragments from a large mammal, probably deer or antelope. These burned fragments were probably from one eroded bone.

One long-bone fragment, burned slightly, was recovered from FN 30. This fragment was from a medium or large mammal (larger than a jackrabbit).

Approximately 50 long-bone shaft fragments, possibly from one eroded bone, were located in FN 33. These fragments appeared to be from a large mammal, probably Artiodactyla.

FN 42 contained seven long-bone shaft fragments, two of which were burned, from a large mammal, probably deer or antelope, and a right innominate fragment from the ischium of a *Sylvilagus* sp. (cottontail rabbit).

INTERPRETATIONS AND CONCLUSIONS

As discussed in the research design, the eight sites investigated during the Fourmile Wash Project should appropriately be treated as subunits of a larger site complex. The smaller sites were similar to one another in terms of content and location, and the Flatiron Site was, in reality, an aggregation of loci, each of which resembled the individual small sites. As referred to by Stone (1988), these sites formed the Fourmile Complex. It is appropriate, then, to focus interpretations on this larger cultural pattern by summarizing the data from each site, then synthesizing and discussing the data with reference to the issues described in the research design.

SITE INTERPRETATIONS

AZ T:5:8(ASM)

This site contained four deflated roasting pits and a very light scatter of lithic artifacts. No subsurface deposits were present at the site. The limited artifactual assemblage suggested that activities at the site had been focused on the processing of wild plant resources. The lack of temporal data precluded an assignment of a specific date to the occupation of the site.

AZ T:5:9(ASM)

This site represented the earliest documented occupation within the project area. Although the major occupation or use of the area seemed to have occurred between A.D. 900 and 1400, the radiocarbon sample taken from Features 8 and 9 yielded a date of 165 B.C.– A.D. 240. The artifacts recovered from this site consisted primarily of nondiagnostic pieces of flaked and ground stone. Two sherds from a Lower Colorado Buff Ware jar also were recovered. These sherds postdated the use of the site that produced the radiocarbon date, since the earliest Lower Colorado Buff Ware ceramics have been dated to after A.D. 700 (Waters 1982).

Most of the features at this site were almost completely eroded away, and surface artifacts were few and not particularly distinctive. The macrobotanical sample analyzed from Features 8 and 9 yielded only small amounts of mesquite and palo verde charcoal. The presence of ground stone tools and the roasting pits indicated that the site had been used for processing wild plant resources. The occupation of the site apparently had occurred during the late Archaic period and perhaps at some time during the Ceramic period.

AZ T:5:10(ASM)

This site consisted of a single rock feature and associated pot break. The rock feature was not well preserved, having been disturbed by a creosote bush. It appeared as an amorphous collection of local cobbles located on a desert pavement ridge on the terrace east of Fourmile Wash. Associated with this feature were the remains of an Aquarius Brown Ware jar, a ceramic type associated with Tizon Brown Ware of the Cerbat tradition (Euler and Dobyns 1958). The dating of this type is rather broad (A.D. 900?–1890), so the assignment of a date of occupation is not possible. The site may well have been associated with historic Upland Yuman use of the area, or the occupation could have been prehistoric (post–A.D. 900?).

Investigators recovered little information relevant to interpretation of site function. The rock feature may have been the remains of a temporary structure or sleeping circle. In all likelihood, this site was a campsite used for a very short period of time by a limited number of people. The camp may have been associated with the exploitation of resources located near Fourmile Wash, or it may have served as a temporary resting place for people traveling through the area.

AZ T:5:11(ASM)

This site appeared to have been used on a limited basis for agricultural purposes and may also have served as a temporary camp. The site consisted of a dispersed group of rock pile features and lithic scatters located on a desert pavement ridge adjacent to Fourmile Wash.

Similar rock piles have been interpreted as agricultural features. The rocks are thought to have retained moisture or to have held poles to which plants could have clung; however, no evidence supporting agricultural use was present in the pollen samples taken from two of these features.

The features were excavated following a night of continuous rain, and the soil under one of the rock piles had become saturated to a greater depth than the surrounding soil, probably because the increased surface volume provided by the rocks captured more runoff within this localized area. This finding may provide support for the suggested agricultural nature of these features.

Artifacts recovered from the site included 24 sherds, most of which were locally produced plainwares, although some Lower Colorado Buff Wares and a single sherd of Wingfield Plain were also identified.   Lithics included flakes and cores produced during reduction episodes.   One handstone made up the ground stone assemblage.

Although the presence of rock piles suggested that agricultural activities had been pursued at this site, investigators recovered no information on the species cultivated. The temporal placement of the occupation could only be narrowed to some time during the prehistoric era.

AZ T:5:12 (ASM), the Flatiron Site

This site consisted of a collection of smaller loci that were, for the most part, quite similar to the materials at the smaller project sites. Several of the loci were, however, relatively complex, containing subsurface deposits and substantial artifact assemblages. The great majority of features investigated consisted of deflated rock piles, roasting pits, and rock clusters, which for the most part yielded very little in the way of subsurface deposits; however, four relatively substantial subsurface features were identified. These features, quite similar to each other in content and morphology, are referred to as occupation surfaces, a term chosen because the features were identifiable as use surfaces upon which activities had been conducted but at which no evidence for a structure could be discerned. These surfaces consisted of hard-packed, ash-stained soil that exhibited flat-lying artifacts and contained cultural features, including roasting pits and small fire pits or hearths. The similarity in form and content of these features indicated that the occupation of the area had been relatively insubstantial and probably characterized by open campsites or perhaps the construction of flimsy structures. The relatively limited artifact density and diversity recognized at these loci supported this conclusion. Activities conducted at the site appeared to have involved the gathering and preparation of wild plant foods, the hunting of game, and most probably the cultivation of corn and amaranths.

AZ T:5:14(ASM)

Four deflated roasting pits were the only features present at this site, none of which contained subsurface deposits. Artifacts were few, consisting of ground and flaked stone. Here again, little can be said other than that it appeared that the site represented activities associated with the gathering and processing of plant foods. Temporal placement of this occupation was not possible.

AZ T:5:16(ASM)

This site was located approximately 600 m east of Fourmile Wash between a small drainage and an area of desert pavement. Three piles of what appeared to be fire-cracked rock were present, but no subsurface deposits were identified. Although three cores had been recorded during the initial survey (Stone 1988), they could not be relocated during the data recovery program.

Based on the scant data recovered, little can be said regarding the function of the site. The probable roasting pits and the lack of artifacts suggested that a small group of people had used the site briefly to process wild plant or, perhaps, animal resources. Any further statements regarding function, temporal placement, or cultural affiliation are unwarranted.

AZ T:5:17(ASM)

With the exception of the Flatiron Site, this was the most substantial site excavated during the project. The site consisted of three surface concentrations of fire-cracked rock, cobbles, and artifacts. A fourth feature, a cluster of cobbles, was purely surficial. One subsurface occupation surface (Feature 5), similar to those unearthed at the Flatiron Site, was also discovered. Data recovered from this feature indicated that deer or antelope and probably rabbit had been cooked on the site. The presence of a mano on the occupation surface and a number of other ground stone items from general site proveniences suggested that plant resources had also been processed there. Unfortunately, neither macrobotanical nor pollen analyses yielded any information concerning the kinds of plant resources processed. The flaked stone assemblage contained a number of small scrapers and a triangular projectile point, artifacts that would have been employed in hunting and preparing game. The ceramic assemblage consisted primarily of material associated with the Lower Colorado Buff Ware tradition (82%), with some locally made ceramics also present (16%). Hohokam wares accounted for only 1% of the assemblage. The dating of this site is uncertain; no material suitable for absolute dating techniques was recovered, and no temporally diagnostic artifacts were present.

GENERAL INTERPRETATIONS

Prehistoric Environment and Subsistence

Information concerning the prehistoric environment of the project area and the subsistence endeavors of its occupants was provided by the analysis of flotation and pollen samples and by the examination of faunal remains. In general, these analyses suggested that the local environment during the occupation of AZ T:5:12(ASM) and AZ T:5:17(ASM) had not drastically differed from what it is now. All of the plant and animal species identified are present in the area today. Tree species included palo verde, mesquite, and ironwood; shrubby species included creosote bush and bursage. Weedy plant types such as chenopods and amaranths, spiderling, globe mallow, and wild sunflower were also present. Animal species associated with the occupation included mule deer, possibly antelope, and jackrabbit. Although the prehistoric natural environment may have varied from that of today in terms of species density or distribution, the overall environmental pattern appears to have been much the same as that of modern times.

The samples analyzed contained only limited evidence for subsistence activities. Use of wild plant species, including chenopods and amaranths, was indicated. The burned remains of examples of these species were identified in both pollen and flotation samples in frequencies suggesting economic utilization. Evidence for use of these plants was indicated in pit features within three occupation surfaces (Occupation Surfaces 1, 2, and 3) at the Flatiron Site. Globe mallow has been used ethnographically both as a medicinal plant and as a food resource (Castetter 1935; Russell 1975); use of this species was indicated for Feature 5 at AZ T:5:17(ASM) and possibly for Feature 103 at the Flatiron Site.

Perhaps the most interesting aspect of the wild plant assemblage was the complete lack of evidence for the use of leguminous resources such as mesquite and palo verde. Wood charcoal and pollen confirmed the presence of these species in the area, and the moist local environment would doubtless have supported abundant stands of these trees. There were, however, no remains of edible plant parts in the samples. The most likely explanation for this situation may be that the area had not been visited during the late summer when these resources would have been available.

Exploitation of animal species was indicated for AZ T:5:17(ASM) and for the Flatiron Site. At the former site, both burned and unburned fragments of either deer or antelope were recovered from the occupation surface (Feature 5). Possible consumption of rabbit was also indicated for this feature. At the Flatiron Site, a pit within Occupation Surface 1 yielded substantial evidence of the preparation of both mule deer and jackrabbit. The cooking of jackrabbits was also indicated for Occupation Surfaces 2 and 4.

Cultivated plant foods were also identified in flotation samples from the Flatiron Site. Corn was recovered from pits within Occupation Surfaces 1, 2, and 4. These remains consisted of cupule, glume, and kernel fragments and were present in very small amounts. Based on the geomorphological characteristics of the area, B. Huckell (Chapter 6) concludes that the area would have been quite suitable for floodwater farming practices. If, in fact, floodwater farming was practiced along Fourmile Wash, the macrofloral and pollen assemblages suggested that corn and possibly chenopods may have been the plants cultivated. The archaeobotanical record at the Flatiron Site was dominated by cheno-ams (96%), with maize accounting for 3.5% of the total estimated number of identified economic plant parts (Chapter 7). The presence of maize kernel and cob fragments suggested that entire cobs had been present and that cultivation of this species may well have occurred at this site. Chenopods produce edible seeds and greens (Gasser 1981:221–22). As B. Huckell suggests (Chapter 6), it is possible that only maize had been cultivated, while cheno-ams had been gathered and eaten by those tending the crops. Domesticated forms of *Amaranthus* and possibly *Chenopodium* have, however, been identified at Hohokam sites (Gasser 1988:226, 228), suggesting that this plant may also have been cultivated.

Chronology

As Stone (1986) has noted, chronological issues in western Arizona are far from resolved, and absolute chronological data from the area are severely lacking. Although the data gathered from the Fourmile excavations are limited, their importance within the regional context is obvious. The majority of the temporally sensitive data were recovered from the Flatiron Site in the form of radiocarbon dates and ceramic materials. One radiocarbon date also was obtained from charcoal collected at AZ T:5:9(ASM). The data from the Flatiron Site consisted of temporally diagnostic ceramic types and radiocarbon dates obtained from samples taken from three occupation surfaces. Table 10.1 illustrates the relationship between the ceramic dates and the radiocarbon dates from the Flatiron Site.

Table 10.1. Chronological Data from the Flatiron Site (AZ T:5:12, ASM)

A.D.	600	700	800	900	1000	1100	1200	1300	1400
Ceramic Dates									
Santa Cruz Red-on-buff									
S. Cruz/Sacaton Red-on-buff									
Sacaton Red-on-buff									
Sacaton Red									
Verde Black-on-gray									
Radiocarbon Dates									
Occupation Surface 4									
Occupation Surface 3									
Occupation Surface 2									

The evidence suggested that the earliest occupation had been limited and that it had occurred during a period equivalent to the late Colonial period of the Hohokam chronology (A.D. 700–900). Evidence for this occupation was derived from a single sherd of Santa Cruz Red-on-buff and a late Santa Cruz/early Sacaton sherd, both recovered from surface contexts. In addition, the early portion of the range for the radiocarbon date for Occupation Surface 4 falls within the Colonial period.

The majority of the evidence indicated that the most intense occupation of the site had occurred during the period between A.D. 900 and 1200. Hohokam Red-on-buff and redwares associated with the Sacaton phase were present, as were Verde Black-on-gray ceramics (Table 10.1). These ceramics all dated to this time period, as did the radiocarbon sample from Occupation Surface 3. The latter half of the date range for Occupation Surface 2 also indicated occupation during this time. The latest occupation was indicated for Occupation Surface 2, which dated to between A.D. 1200 and 1400. As Vokes (Chapter 5) notes, the buffware ceramics from the Flatiron Site most closely resembled the Lower Gila Series of the Lower Colorado Buff Ware tradition (Schroeder 1958). This material is considered to postdate A.D. 1150.

In summary, the limited data suggest that the Flatiron Site was used to a modest degree during the late Colonial period, most intensively during the period between A.D. 900 and 1200, and again, to a lesser extent, between A.D. 1200 and 1400. It should be kept in mind that the occupation of the Flatiron Site was characterized by repeated short-term occupations and that these dates represent short segments of time within a larger unknown temporal framework.

The only other chronological data recovered from the project area was a radiocarbon date from AZ T:5:9(ASM). The analyzed sample was taken from the fill of a roasting pit and yielded a date between 165 B.C. and A.D. 240. This result indicated that the site had been occupied either in the Archaic period or during the transitional period between the Archaic and the early Ceramic periods. No temporally diagnostic artifacts were present at the site. The presence of two plainware sherds of Patayan II affinity may cast doubt on the validity of the radiocarbon date or, more likely, represent a later, limited reoccupation of the site (Waters 1982).

Cultural Relationships

Prehistoric western Arizona has been described as a frontier region, a sparsely populated transitional zone characterized by cultural mixing or joint use (Stone 1986). In west-central Arizona, the significance of zones of ceramic intermixture has been a research issue in a number of studies (Carrico and Quillen 1982; Dobyns 1974; Stone 1982) that have attempted to determine whether this mixed zone represented social interaction or the simultaneous or sequential use of the area by groups from surrounding culture areas. Although some studies have concluded that these materials represented the use of the area by neighboring groups (Dobyns 1974; Stein 1981), other research has suggested that an indigenous group resided within this area as a homeland (Schroeder 1957).

The data base for the area surrounding the project area, like that of much of western Arizona, lacks basic information concerning site type, distribution, and content. An examination of the limited data for the area surrounding the project area is, however, instructive.

Sites have been investigated in the Palo Verde Hills to the south of the project area (Stein 1981). The Palo Verde pattern (Stone 1986) consists of "a series of small but relatively complex loci consisting of rock concentrations (possible hearths or roasting pits) with associated ceramics, flaked stone artifacts and manufacturing debris, and grinding implements. Ceramics, not present at all sites, incorporate a diverse range of types associated with Hohokam and Patayan wares" (Stone 1988:29). Activities conducted at these sites are thought to have been diverse, including hunting and gathering and possibly floodwater farming (Stein 1981).

Based on the results of the Granite Reef Aqueduct Survey (Brown and Stone 1982), Stone (1986) defined the Granite Reef pattern, which apparently characterizes the upper bajada areas north of the present project area. This pattern is one of low site density, with sites consisting of small lithic scatters and rock rings, alignments, and concentrations. Some of these sites may have been temporary camps.

The BLM White Tanks West Survey was a sample survey of BLM lands between the Big Horn Mountains and the Hassayampa River, which confirmed the previously defined pattern of low archaeological site density in the Tonopah Desert (Stone 1988). Of the 51 sites identified, 38 were located along Fourmile Wash and near Flatiron Mountain. With the exception of the sites in the Fourmile Wash area, these sites were all rock rings, concentrations, and alignments similar to sites recorded during the Granite Reef Survey (Brown and Stone 1982). Ceramics at these sites included both Hohokam and Lower Colorado series.

The survey data illustrate the unusual nature of the sites along Fourmile Wash. Although the surrounding region exhibits a markedly low site density, the Fourmile Wash area is characterized by relatively high site density. Thus, the project area stands out as a locus of relatively intense occupation within a little-used larger region. Curiously, this sparsely inhabited area is located little more than 20 overland miles (32 km) from large, contemporaneous riverine Hohokam villages in the western Phoenix basin and only 15 miles (24 km) north of the Gila River.

The presence of Hohokam sherds and the proximity of many areas in the western desert to riverine locales has led researchers to suggest that the pattern of seemingly mixed assemblages represents the periodic use of the desert areas by riverine groups. The data from the project suggest that the sites were inhabited by local populations that were not Hohokam. As Vokes (Chapter 5) has demonstrated, only 10% of the ceramics recovered from the project sites were derived from the Hohokam tradition. Most significantly, the majority of the ceramics at the Flatiron Site were locally made brown plainwares. Lower Colorado Buff Wares were also well represented, and the local ceramics bore more resemblance to these materials than to Hohokam wares. It is important to note that in several cases these types co-occurred in sealed feature proveniences (Features 28, 45, 85 [Table 5.3]), thereby demonstrating their contemporaneity and strengthening the argument that these materials represented a discrete assemblage.

Previous researchers have suggested that interdrainage desert occupations by riverine farming groups could be recognized by greater specialization in site types and artifact assemblages (Doelle 1980; Rice and Dobbins 1981). This approach is based on the assumption that riverine groups planned expeditions into the area to exploit specific resources using specialized tool kits and task groups. As has been discussed, the assemblages from the Fourmile Wash sites were anything but specialized, consisting of expediently produced and minimally utilized flaked and ground stone tools. This pattern suggests that these materials were produced by mobile groups that did not carry tools with them but instead used locally available materials and expended little effort in manufacture, discarding tools where they were made and utilized.

Given the ceramic data, it is suggested that at least the southeastern portion of the western Arizona desert was occupied by peoples who were distinct from those of the surrounding region. The mixed artifact assemblages were not deposited by nonlocal groups in subsequent visits but in fact represent the material culture of the local inhabitants.

Given the proposition that there was a local population, what can be said concerning the range of variability in this group's subsistence activities? Ceramic assemblages similar to that identified along Fourmile Wash have been reported to the northwest of the project area (Stone 1986:83). These assemblages were composed of brownware (which may have been locally produced), Lower Colorado Buff Ware, Prescott Gray Ware, Hohokam Red-on-buff, and intrusive decorated types from northern Arizona. This assemblage seems to occur in an area that includes the McMullen and Aguila valleys, which lie between the Harquahala and Harcuvar Mountains in the vicinity of Aguila, Arizona. The area has relatively abundant water, and known site types include rock shelters and what appear to be base camps. Stone (1986) speculates that this area may have been a zone of multiple frontiers from which indigenous groups interacted with the neighboring Hohokam and Prescott populations.

This area is less than 35 miles (56 km) from the project area via Jackrabbit Wash and less than 50 miles (80 km) away along Centennial Wash. Stone's assertion would thus appear to be consistent with the data from the Fourmile Wash Project. It is suggested here that the sites along Fourmile Wash may have been associated with those within the area described by Stone, and that these sites were associated with a local population. If this is the case, then the current project area represents the southeastern range of the groups that produced these sites. Data from the sites in the Palo Verde Hills to the south of the project area has led Stein (1981) to conclude that they were occupied by Hohokam groups. And, as noted, large sedentary riverine Hohokam villages were located only 20 miles (32 km) southeast of the project area. Although the western range of this local group is unknown, it appears to have extended at least to the Harcuvar Mountains. The affinities of the locally produced ceramics at the Flatiron Site with the Lower Colorado Buff Ware tradition reflect this western orientation. The Lower Colorado wares at the site may well have entered the domain of these people from the western area. It may be more than coincidental that during the Historic period, the area extending from the project area south to the Palo Verde Hills was an unoccupied boundary area separating the agricultural Maricopa on the south from the hunter-gatherer Yavapai on the north (Schroeder 1974).

The proposition that portions of western Arizona were inhabited by an indigenous group has previously been proposed by Schroeder (1957, 1979). His Hakataya model proposes that much of central and western Arizona was populated by indigenous groups descended from local Archaic populations. The Hakataya are also seen as the forebears of the Yavapai. This model has been criticized for being overly general (McGuire and Schiffer 1982), and other researchers have provided different approaches to the culture history of this region (Euler and Green 1978; Pilles 1981). Although the data from the present project are not sufficient to fully resolve the arguments concerning cultural developments in western Arizona, they add substantially to an understanding of the nature of the occupation of the area.

This is not to say that all sites along Fourmile Wash are representative of a single homogeneous population. It is quite possible that sites such as AZ T:5:17(ASM) and AZ T:5:10(ASM) were in fact produced by riverine groups visiting or moving through the area. What is important is the fact that the project data provide strong evidence in support of the contention that there was a local population residing within this area that was distinct from the populations of the surrounding region.

Settlement Pattern and Social Organization

Previous researchers have defined three major land-use models that can be applied to the desert areas of western Arizona (Brown and Stone 1982; Doelle 1980). These are (1) temporary or seasonal use of desert resources by river-based groups, probably farmers; (2) occupation by mobile groups that relied primarily or exclusively on wild resources; and (3) travel and associated temporary resource use. Although these patterns may have varied and were not necessarily mutually exclusive, the presence of a local population within the region suggests that the model most applicable to the area would be one that is similar to Kroeber's (1920) Upland Yuman or Yavapai subsistence model. The Yavapai were highly mobile hunter-gatherers who followed an annual subsistence cycle and planted crops periodically at favorable locations. As Stone described them, "The Yavapai depended on wild resources, most of which were available seasonally. The entire tribal range included pine forests, juniper-oak woodlands, chaparral, desert, and riparian zones yielding a variety of resources. Local bands varied in specifics of scheduling and use of particular resources, but bands of all subtribes had access to several environmental zones" (Stone 1988:41).

The seasonal availability of resources over a wide geographical range required a great degree of mobility. Small groups of people, usually consisting of up to ten nuclear or extended families (Gifford 1936:271), occupied a series of temporary or seasonal base camps.

B. Huckell (Chapter 6) has described the geomorphological attributes that may have drawn prehistoric populations to the area. As he notes, the area was relatively moist, supported comparatively lush vegetation, and was suitable for floodwater farming. Evidence from the Flatiron Site and from AZ T:5:17(ASM) indicated that occupation surfaces represented camp areas used by a limited number of individuals for relatively brief periods of time. The insubstantial nature of the features, the limited range of artifact types, the expediency of production visible in the lithic assemblage, and the lack of substantial refuse deposits all support this interpretation. The lack of evidence for architectural features also suggests a relatively short occupation. It is known, however, that the Western Yavapai constructed domed huts with a framework of willow, ocotillo, or mesquite thatched with grass (Gifford 1936:271). Little indication of such ephemeral structures would remain.

Although the size of the social groups that periodically occupied the sites is difficult to estimate, the range of artifacts, including shell and stone jewelry, ceramics, stone grinding tools, and projectile points, suggests that relatively complete social groups were present. What emerges is a pattern of relatively substantial occupations for periods of time probably ranging from several weeks to an entire growing season. Evidence for the period of the year during which the sites were occupied is limited to the archaeobotanical remains from three sites. Cheno-ams are available from the early spring to late summer, but as Fish (Chapter 8) notes, chenopods and amaranths are generally not gathered in the earlier spring months. The aggregates of globe mallow pollen at the Flatiron Site would indicate a summer occupation, although this plant tends to bloom opportunistically according to available moisture. The cultivation of corn through floodwater farming would also suggest an occupation during the summer months. It is curious, however, to note the complete lack of evidence for the exploitation of mesquite and other summer-ripening legumes, which were staple foods of many prehistoric groups.

The Yavapai planted crops in favorable areas and then left to exploit wild resources, returning again for the harvest (Mariella 1983). It may well be that prehistoric inhabitants followed a similar schedule, occupying the project area both before and after mesquite and other legumes were available but not during the times when those beans should have been gathered.

In summary, the sites in the project area are interpreted as representing the remains produced by relatively mobile groups during a seasonal round of resource exploitation activities.

Some of the less substantial project sites probably were short-term camps at which a limited range of activities occurred. The occupation surfaces at the Flatiron Site and at AZ T:5:17(ASM) probably indicate more substantial occupations lasting up to several months and involving a broader range of activities, including agriculture. Since so little is known of the range of site types in the larger region, it is difficult to add much to our understanding of the overall subsistence pattern. It would appear, however, that the Flatiron Site represents a relatively substantial and complex occupation, having served from time to time as a base camp. Other substantial sites are likely to exist in particularly favorable locations within the region.

External Relationships

The material culture recovered from the Fourmile Wash sites clearly indicates contact with neighboring groups. Hohokam materials included a variety of both plain and decorated ceramics and shell and stone jewelry. Materials from the Prescott region and elsewhere in northern Arizona included Verde Black-on-gray ceramics and northern Arizona whitewares. The Lower Colorado region was also well represented in the ceramic assemblage.

Historically, the Yuman tribes participated in wide-ranging trade networks that incorporated numerous groups in the Southwest, southern California, and northern Mexico (Davis 1963; Forbes 1965; Gifford 1936; Spier 1970). The extensive trail systems throughout western Arizona were doubtless associated with these networks. Exchange systems included both the direct and indirect movement of materials over long distances. Exchange between river and Upland Yuman groups typified a general pattern of farmer/hunter-gatherer trade, that is, the exchange of cultivated foods and manufactured goods for animal products and wild resources (Davis 1961; Kroeber 1935; Peterson 1978).

This trade model appears similar to the picture presented by the Fourmile data. Obviously the inhabitants of this region had access to materials from the areas adjacent to them, although the goods exchanged and the mechanisms through which this exchange occurred cannot be identified. What is important is that these materials represent trade introduction into the area, not use of the area by surrounding groups.

SUMMARY AND CONCLUSIONS

The data suggest that the project sites were occupied primarily between A.D. 900 and 1150, although the project area was occupied at least as early as the Archaic period and as late as A.D. 1400. The eight sites investigated probably represent loci utilized in a variety of subsistence activities during the seasonal round of a local population. These activities included the gathering and processing of wild plant resources and the hunting and consumption of game animals such as deer and rabbit. In addition, relatively unique local geomorphological conditions produced a situation that was quite amenable to the application of floodwater farming techniques. The presence of maize and chenopod remains in the macrobotanical assemblage indicates that these species may well have been cultivated by site inhabitants.

The most significant conclusions drawn from the project data concern the nature of the groups that occupied these sites. Analysis of ceramics indicated that the project area and the region to the northwest of it had been inhabited by local populations that had made brown plainware and redware ceramics. Intrusive materials within the ceramic assemblage included Hohokam wares, Lower Colorado Buff Wares, and Prescott Gray Ware, which had been obtained through trade with neighboring groups.

This contention would seem to support Schroeder's (1957, 1979) model of cultural development, at least for western Arizona. Schroeder proposed that these local populations had descended from local Archaic groups and that they had been the prehistoric antecedents of the Yavapai. The current data do not lend themselves to a resolution of these aspects of the model. They do, however, clearly indicate that the cultural materials were produced by the activities of a resident population and not left behind during occasional forays into the desert conducted by people from surrounding riverine- adapted Hohokam or Patayan groups. Although the data from the present project are not sufficient to fully resolve the arguments concerning cultural developments in western Arizona, they can serve as a basis upon which future research may more fruitfully be based.

APPENDIX

RADIOCARBON SAMPLES

Earl W. Sires

Four radiocarbon samples were submitted to Beta Analytic, Inc., of Coral Gables, Florida. All were wood charcoal samples recovered from excavated proveniences. Two samples were identified as mesquite (*Prosopis*), and the other two were identified as possibly mesquite. Three samples were from the Flatiron Site (AZ T:5:12, ASM), and the fourth specimen was from AZ T:5:9(ASM). The results were tree-ring corrected using the calibration date tables computed by Klein et al. (1982). The corrected results are presented in Table B.1.

Table B.1. Radiocarbon Results.

Lab No.	Field No.	Feature	C14	Calibrated
26452	T:5:9-20	9	1920 +/- 80 B.P.	165 B.C.–A.D. 240
26453	T:5:12-126	103	720 +/- 90 B.P.	A.D. 1180–1400
26454	T:5:12-152	113	1120 +/- 50 B.P.	A.D. 775–1030
26455	T:5:12-159	111	1020 +/- 100 B.P.	A.D. 860–1225

REFERENCES

Antieau, John M., and David H. Greenwald
1981 Material Culture: Stone. In *The Palo Verde Archaeological Investigations. Hohokam Settlement at the Confluence: Excavations along the Palo Verde Pipeline*, edited by John M. Antieau. Research Papers No. 20. Museum of Northern Arizona, Flagstaff.

Beaglehole, Ernest
1937 *Notes on Hopi Economic Life.* Yale University Publications in Anthropology No. 15. Yale University Press, New Haven.

Bean, Lowell John, and Katherine Siva Saubel
1972 *Temalpakh: Cahuilla Indian Knowledge and Use of Plants.* Malki Museum Press, Banning, California.

Bohrer, Vorsila L., and Karen R. Adams
1977 *Ethnobotanical Techniques and Approaches at Salmon Ruin, New Mexico.* Contributions in Anthropology No. 8(1). Eastern New Mexico University, Portales.

Bostwick, Todd W.
1984 An Archaeological Survey of Reaches 1 and 2, Upper Westside Canal and Centennial Levee, Maricopa County Flood Control District and Harquahala Valley Irrigation District, Central Arizona Project. MS on file, Northland Research, Flagstaff.

1988 *An Investigation of Archaic Subsistence and Settlement in the Harquahala Valley, Maricopa County, Arizona.* Northland Research, Flagstaff.

Breternitz, David A.
1966 *An Appraisal of Tree-Ring Dated Pottery in the Southwest.* Anthropological Papers of the University of Arizona No. 10. University of Arizona Press, Tucson.

Brown, Patricia E., and Connie L. Stone, editors
1982 *Granite Reef: A Study in Desert Archaeology.* Anthropological Research Papers No. 28. Arizona State University, Tempe.

Bryan, Kirk
1929 Floodwater Farming. *Geographical Review* 19:444–56.

Carrico, Richard L., and Dennis K. Quillen
1982 *Cultural Resource Inventory and National Register Assessment of the Southern California Edison Palo Verde to Devers Transmission Line Corridor (Arizona Portion).* WESTEC Services, San Diego. Submitted to Southern California Edison, Rosemead.

Castetter, Edward F.
1935 *Ethnobiological Studies in the American Southwest I: Uncultivated Native Plants Used as Sources of Food.* Bulletin No. 266; Biological Series vol. 4, No. 1. University of New Mexico, Albuquerque.

Castetter, Edward F., and Willis H. Bell
1942 *Pima and Papago Agriculture.* Inter-American Studies No. 1. University of New Mexico Press, Albuquerque.

Castetter, Edward F., and Willis H. Bell

1951 *Yuman Indian Agriculture.* University of New Mexico Press, Albuquerque.

Castetter, Edward F., and Ruth Underhill

1935 *Ethnobiological Studies in the American Southwest II: The Ethnobiology of the Papago Indians.* Bulletin No. 275; Biological Series, Vol. 4, No. 3. University of New Mexico, Albuquerque.

Clotts, H.

1917 *History of the Papago Indians and History of Irrigation, Papago Indian Reservations, Arizona.* U.S. Indian Service, Washington, D.C.

Crown, Patricia L.

1981 Analysis of the Las Colinas Ceramics. In *The 1968 Excavations at Mound 8, Las Colinas Ruin Group, Phoenix, Arizona*, edited by L. C. Hammack and A. P. Sullivan, pp. 87–169. Archaeological Series No. 154. Arizona State Museum. The University of Arizona, Tucson.

Curtin, L. S. M.

1984 *By the Prophet of the Earth: Ethnobotany of the Pima.* University of Arizona Press, Tucson.

Cushing, Frank Hamilton

1920 *Zuni Breadstuff.* Museum of the American Indian, Heye Foundation, New York.

Davis, Emma Lou

1963 The Desert Culture of the Western Great Basin: A Lifeway of Seasonal Transhumance. *American Antiquity* 29:202–12.

Davis, Emma Lou, Kathryn H. Brown, and Jaqueline Nichols

1980 *Evaluation of Early Human Activities and Remains in the California Desert.* Great Basin Foundation, Riverside, California.

Davis, James T.

1961 *Trade Routes and Economic Exchange among the Indians of California.* University of California Archaeological Survey Reports No. 54. Berkeley.

Dobyns, Henry F.

1974 *Prehistoric Indian Occupation within the Eastern Area of the Yuman Complex.* Garland Press, New York.

Doebley, John F.

1984 "Seeds" of Wild Grasses: A Major Food of Southwestern Indians. *Economic Botany* 38(1):52–64.

Doelle, William H.

1980 *Past Adaptive Patterns in Western Papagueria: An Archaeological Study of Nonriverine Resource Use.* Unpublished Ph.D. dissertation, Department of Anthropology, The University of Arizona, Tucson.

Doyel, David E., and Mark D. Elson
1985 *Hohokam Settlement and Economic Systems in the Central New River Drainage, Arizona.* Soil Systems Publications in Archaeology No. 4. Soil Systems, Phoenix.

Doyel, David E., and Fred T. Plog, editors
1980 *Current Issues in Hohokam Prehistory: Proceedings of a Symposium.* Anthropological Research Papers No. 23. Arizona State University, Tempe.

Elmore, Francis H.
1944 *Ethnobotany of the Navajo.* Monograph No. 8. School of American Research, Santa Fe.

Euler, Robert C., and Henry F. Dobyns
1958 Tizon Brown Ware. In *Pottery Types of the Southwest*, edited by Harold S. Colton. Museum of Northern Arizona Ceramic Series 3D. Northern Arizona Society of Science and Art, Flagstaff.

Euler, Robert C., and Dee F. Green
1978 *An Archaeological Reconnaissance of Middle Havasu Canyon, Arizona.* Cultural Resources Report No. 22, U.S. Forest Service, Southwestern Region, Albuquerque.

Felger, Richard F., and Mary Beck Moser
1985 *People of the Desert and Sea: Ethnobiology of the Seri Indians.* University of Arizona Press, Tucson.

Fish, Suzanne K.
1984 Salt-Gila Aqueduct Project Pollen Analysis. In *Hohokam Archaeology along the Salt-Gila Aqueduct*, vol. 7, edited by Lynn S. Teague and Patricia L. Crown, pp. 9–16. Archaeological Series No. 150. Arizona State Museum, Tucson.

1985 Prehistoric Disturbance Floras of the Lower Sonoran Desert and Their Implications. In *Late Quaternary Vegetation and Climates of the American Southwest*, edited by B. Jacob, P. Fall, and O. Davis. American Association of Stratigraphic Palynologists Contribution Series No. 16. Houston, Texas.

Forbes, Jack D.
1965 *Warriors of the Colorado.* University of Oklahoma Press, Norman.

Ford, Karen Cowan
1975 *Las Yerbas de la Gente: A Study of Hispano-American Medicinal Plants.* Anthropological Papers of the Museum of Anthropology No. 60. University of Michigan, Ann Arbor.

Fuller, Steven L.
1973 *Archaeological Clearance Investigations at the Gillespie Dam, Palo Verde Hills, and Indian Buttes Plant Siting Locations.* Museum of Northern Arizona, Flagstaff. Submitted to Arizona Public Service, Phoenix; Salt River Project, Phoenix, and Tucson Gas & Electric, Tucson.

Gasser, Robert E.
1981 Hohokam Use of Desert Plant Foods. *Desert Plants* 3(4):216–34.

Gasser, Robert E.
1982 Hohokam Use of Desert Food Plants. *Desert Plants* 2:216–34.

1987 Macrofloral Remains. In *Environmental and Subsistence. The Archaeology of the San Xavier Bridge Site (AZ BB:13:14) Tucson Basin, Southern Arizona*, edited by John C. Ravesloot, pp. 303–13. Archaeological Series No. 171. Arizona State Museum, Tucson.

1988 Flotation Studies. In *Environment and Subsistence, vol. 5 of Hohokam Settlement along the Slopes of the Picacho Mountains*, edited by Donald E. Weaver, Jr., pp. 143–235. Research Paper No. 35. Museum of Northern Arizona, Flagstaff.

Gasser, Robert E., and Charles Miksicek
1985 The Specialists: A Reappraisal of Hohokam Exchange and the Archaeobotanical Record. In *Proceedings of the 1983 Hohokam Symposium*, part 2, edited by Alfred Dittert and Donald Dove, pp. 483–97. Occasional Papers No. 2. Arizona Archaeological Society, Phoenix.

Gifford, E. W.
1936 *Northeastern and Western Yavapai*. Publications in American Archaeology and Ethnology 34:247–354. University of California, Berkeley.

Greenhouse, R., R. E. Gasser, and J. W. Gish
1981 Cholla Bud Roasting Pits: An Ethnoarchaeological Example. *The Kiva* 46:227–42.

Gregory, David A.
1987 *The Archaeology of the Alamo Lake Area*. Statistical Research Technical Series No. 13. Report prepared for the Los Angeles District, U.S. Army Corps of Engineers, Los Angeles.

Haas, Pamela
1973 *A Preliminary Draft for Phase I Archaeological and Ethnohistorical Research Consultation for Proposed Power Line Corridors*. Museum of Northern Arizona, Flagstaff. Submitted to Arizona Public Service, Phoenix, and Salt River Project, Phoenix.

Hack, John T.
1942 *The Changing Physical Environment of the Hopi Indians of Arizona*. Papers of the Peabody Museum of American Archaeology and Ethnology No. 24(1). Harvard University, Cambridge.

Haury, Emil W.
1937 Shell. In *Excavations at Snaketown: Material Culture*, by Harold S. Gladwin, Emil W. Haury, E. B. Sayles, and Nora Gladwin, pp. 135–53. Medallion Papers No. 25. Gila Pueblo, Globe.

1950 *The Stratigraphy and Archaeology of Ventana Cave*. 2d ed. University of Arizona Press, Tucson.

1976 *The Hohokam: Desert Farmers & Craftsmen*. University of Arizona Press, Tucson.

Hayden, Julian D.
1976 Pre-Altithermal Archaeology in the Sierra Pinacate, Sonora, Mexico. *American Antiquity* 41:274–89.

Haynes, C. Vance, Jr.
1980 Paleoindian Charcoal from Meadowcroft Rockshelter: Is Contamination a Problem? *American Antiquity* 45:582–88.

Hevly, Richard, Paul S. Martin, and H. G. Yocum
1965 Studies of the Modern Pollen Rain in the Sonoran Desert. *Journal of the Arizona Academy of Sciences* 3:123–25.

Hubbard, R. N. L. B.
1980 Development of Agriculture in Europe and the Near East: Evidence from Quantitative Studies. *Economic Botany* 34(1):51–67.

Huckell, Bruce B.
1979 *The Coronet Real Project: Archaeological Investigations on the Luke Range, Southwestern Arizona.* Archaeological Series No. 129. Arizona State Museum, Tucson.

1984 The Paleo-Indian and Archaic Occupation of the Tucson Basin: An Overview. *The Kiva* 49:133–45.

Huckell, Lisa W.
1986 Botanical Remains. In *Excavations at the Hodges Site, Pima County, Arizona*, edited by Robert W. Layhe, pp. 241–69. Archaeological Series No. 170. Arizona State Museum, Tucson.

Irwin-Williams, Cynthia
1967 Picosa: The Elementary Southwestern Culture. *American Antiquity* 32:441–57.

1979 Post-Pleistocene Archaeology, 7000–2000 B.C. In *Southwest*, edited by Alfonso Ortiz, pp. 31–42. *Handbook of North American Indians*, vol. 9. Smithsonian Institution, Washington, D.C.

Jennings, Jesse D.
1957 *Danger Cave.* Society for American Archaeology Memoir No. 14. Washington, D.C.

Johnson, Alfred E.
1963 *An Appraisal of the Archaeological Resources of Five Regional Parks in Maricopa County, Arizona.* Arizona State Museum, Tucson. Submitted to Maricopa County Parks and Recreation Commission, Phoenix.

Kearney, Thomas H., and Robert H. Peebles
1964 *Arizona Flora.* 2d ed. University of California, Berkeley.

Klein, Jeffery, J. C. Lerman, P. E. Damon, and E. K. Ralph
1982 Calibration of Radiocarbon Dates: Tables Based on the Consensus Data of the Workshop on Calibrating the Radiocarbon Time Scale. *Radiocarbon* 24(2):103–50.

Kroeber, Alfred L.
1920 *Yuman Tribes of the Lower Colorado River*, pp. 475–85. Publications in American Archaeology and Ethnology No. 16. University of California, Berkeley.

Kroeber, Alfred L.
    1935 *Walapai Ethnography*. Memoirs of the American Anthropological Association No. 42.
    Menasha, Wisconsin.

McGee, William J.
    1898 Papagueria. *The National Geographic Magazine* 9(8):346–71.

McGuire, Randall H., and Michael B. Schiffer, editors
    1982 *Hohokam and Patayan: Prehistory of Southwestern Arizona*. Academic Press, New York.

Mariella, Patricia S.
    1983 *The Political Economy of Federal Resettlement Policies in Native American Communities:
    The Fort McDowell Yavapai Case*. Unpublished Ph.D. dissertation, Department of
    Anthropology, Arizona State University, Tempe.

Mariella, Patricia S., and Sigrid Khera
    1983 Yavapai. In *Southwest*, edited by Alfonso Ortiz, pp. 38–54. *Handbook of North American
    Indians*, vol. 10. Smithsonian Institution, Washington, D.C.

Martin, Paul Schultz
    1963 *The Last 10,000 Years: A Fossil Pollen Record of the American Southwest*. University of
    Arizona Press, Tucson.

Martin, Paul Sidney, and Fred Plog
    1973 *The Archaeology of Arizona*. Doubleday/Natural History Press, Garden City, N.Y.

Meals for Millions/Freedom from Hunger Foundation
    1980 *O'odham I:waki, Wild Greens of the Desert People*. Meals for Millions, Freedom from
    Hunger Foundation, Tucson.

Mehringer, Peter J.
    1967 Pollen Analysis of the Tule Springs Area, Nevada. In *Pleistocene Studies in Southern
    Nevada*, edited by H. Marie Wormington and Dorothy Ellis, pp. 130–200. Anthropological
    Papers No. 13. Nevada State Museum, Carson City.

Miksicek, Charles H.
    1984 Historic Desertification, Prehistoric Vegetation Change, and Hohokam Subsistence in the
    Salt-Gila Basin. In *Environmental and Subsistence, vol. 7 of Hohokam Archaeology along
    the Salt-Gila Aqueduct*, edited by Lynn S. Teague and Patricia L. Crown, pp. 53–80.
    Archaeological Series No. 150. Arizona State Museum, Tucson.

Nabhan, Gary
    1983 *Papago Fields: Arid Lands Ethnobotany and Agricultural Ecology*. Unpublished Ph.D.
    dissertation, Department of Arid Lands Resource Sciences, University of Arizona, Tucson.

National Research Council
    1984 *Amaranth: Modern Prospects for an Ancient Crop*. National Academy Press, Washington,
    D.C.

Parker, Kittie F.
    1972 *An Illustrated Guide to Arizona Weeds*. University of Arizona Press, Tucson.

Peterson, Jean Treloggen
1978 Hunter-Gatherer/Farmer Exchange. *American Anthropologist* 80:335–51.

Pilles, Peter J., Jr.
1981 The Southern Sinagua. *Plateau* 53(1):6–17.

Rice, Glen E., and Edward Dobbins
1981 *Prehistoric Community Patterns in the Western Desert of Arizona.* Anthropological Field Studies No. 2. Arizona State University, Tempe.

Robbins, Wilfred W., John P. Harrington, and Barbara Freire-Marreco
1916 *Ethnobiology of the Tewa Indians.* Bureau of American Ethnology Bulletin No. 55. Smithsonian Institution, Washington, D.C.

Rogers, Malcom J.
n.d. Personal Field Notes and Maps. On file at the Museum of Man, San Diego, and the U.S. Bureau of Land Management, Phoenix.

1945 An Outline of Yuman Prehistory. *Southwest Journal of Anthropology* 1:167–98.

1958 San Dieguito Implements from the Terraces of the Rincon, Pantano, and Rillito Drainage System. *The Kiva* 24:1–23.

1966 *Ancient Hunters of the Far West*, edited by Richard F. Pourade. Union-Tribune Publishing, San Diego.

Russell, Frank
1975 *The Pima Indians.* Reprint. University of Arizona Press, Tucson. Originally published 1908, in *Twenty-sixth Annual Report of the Bureau of American Ethnology*, 1904–1905. U.S. Government Printing Office, Washington, D.C.

Saul, William Emmet
1955 *A Descriptive Catalogue of the Trees and Larger Woody Shrubs of Utah Based on the Anatomy of the Wood.* Unpublished Ph.D. dissertation, Department of Botany, University of Utah, Salt Lake City.

Sayles, E. B., and Ernst Antevs
1941 *The Cochise Culture.* Medallion Papers No. 29. Gila Pueblo, Globe.

Schoenwetter, James, and Larry Doerschlag
1971 Surficial Pollen Records from Central Arizona I: Sonoran Desert Scrub. *Journal of the Arizona Academy of Science* 6:216–21.

Schroeder, Albert H.
1957 The Hakataya Cultural Tradition. *American Antiquity* 23:176–78.

1958 Lower Colorado Buff Ware. In *Pottery Types of the Southwest*, edited by Harold S. Colton. Museum of Northern Arizona Ceramic Series 3D. Northern Arizona Society of Science and Art, Flagstaff.

Schroeder, Albert H.
1974 *A Study of Yavapai History.* American Indian Ethnohistory: Indians of the Southwest. Garland Publishing, New York.

1979 Prehistory: Hakataya. In *Southwest*, edited by Alfonso Ortiz, pp. 100–7. *Handbook of North American Indians*, vol. 9. Smithsonian Institution, Washington, D.C.

Schumm, S. A., and R. F. Hadley
1957 Arroyos and the Semiarid Cycle of Erosion. *American Journal of Science* 255:161–74.

Sires, Earl W., and David A. Gregory
1988 Proposal for Archaeological Testing at Nine Sites in the BLM Lower Gila-White Tanks West Project Area. MS on file, U.S. Bureau of Land Management, Phoenix District Office, Phoenix.

Spier, Leslie
1970 *Yuman Tribes of the Gila River.* Reprint. Cooper Square Publishers, New York.

Stein, Pat
1976 *Palo Verde Nuclear Generating Station. Phase II Investigations for the Realignment of Wintersburg Road as an Access Route to the Plant Site Facility.* Museum of Northern Arizona, Flagstaff. Submitted to Arizona Public Service, Phoenix; Salt River Project, Phoenix; and Southern California Edison, Rosemead, California.

1981 *The Palo Verde Archaeological Investigations.* Anthropological Research Paper No. 21. Museum of Northern Arizona, Flagstaff.

1988 *Homesteading in the Depression: A Study of Two Short-lived Homesteads in the Harquahala Valley, Arizona.* Northland Research, Flagstaff.

Stevenson, Matilda Coxe
1915 Ethnobotany of the Zuni Indians. In *Thirtieth Annual Report of the Bureau of American Ethnology, 1908–1909*, pp. 31–102. U.S. Government Printing Office, Washington, D.C.

Stone, Connie L.
1982 An Examination of Ceramic Variability in Western Arizona. In *Granite Reef: A Study in Desert Archaeology*, edited by Patricia E. Brown and Connie L. Stone, pp. 99–136. Anthropological Research Papers No. 28. Arizona State University, Tempe.

1986 *Deceptive Desolation: Prehistory of the Sonoran Desert in West Central Arizona.* Cultural Resource Series No. 1. U.S. Bureau of Land Management, Arizona State Office, Phoenix.

1988 *Human Use of the Tonopah Desert: The White Tanks West Project.* U.S. Bureau of Land Management, Phoenix District Office, Phoenix.

Sullivan, Alan P., and Kenneth C. Rozen
1985 Debitage Analysis and Archaeological Interpretation. *American Antiquity* 50:755–79.

Swarthout, Jeanne
1981 *An Archaeological Overview for the Lower Colorado River Valley, Arizona, Nevada, and California.* 4 vols. Museum of Northern Arizona, Flagstaff. Submitted to U.S. Bureau of Reclamation, Boulder City, Nevada.

Teague, Lynn S., Susan A. Brew, and Bruce B. Huckell
1982 *Arizona State Museum Cultural Resource Management Division Data Recovery Manual.* Arizona State Museum Archaeological Series No. 158. The University of Arizona, Tucson.

Trott, J. James
1974 *Final Report for Phase II Investigations for Selecting Water Line, Railroad, and Plant Access Routes.* Museum of Northern Arizona, Flagstaff. Submitted to Arizona Public Service, Phoenix; Salt River Project; Phoenix, and Tucson Gas & Electric, Tucson.

Vestal, Paul A.
1952 *Ethnobotany of the Ramah Navajo.* Papers of the Peabody Museum of American Archaeology and Ethnology No. 40(4). Harvard University, Cambridge.

Vokes, Arthur W.
1984 The Shell Assemblage of the Salt-Gila Aqueduct Project Sites. In *Material Culture, vol. 8 of Hohokam Archaeology along the Salt-Gila Aqueduct, Central Arizona Project,* edited by Lynn S. Teague and Patricia L. Crown, pp. 467–574. Archaeological Series No. 150. Arizona State Museum, Tucson.

Warren, Claude N.
1967 The San Dieguito Complex: A Review and Hypothesis. *American Antiquity* 32:168–85.

Wasley, William W., and Alfred E. Johnson
1965 *Salvage Archaeology in Painted Rocks Reservoir, Western Arizona.* University of Arizona Anthropological Papers No. 9. University of Arizona Press, Tucson.

Waters, Michael R.
1982 The Lowland Patayan Ceramic Tradition. In *Hohokam and Patayan: Prehistory of Southwestern Arizona,* edited by Randall H. McGuire and Michael B. Schiffer, pp. 275–97. Academic Press, New York.

1987 Geomorphic Investigations of the Bajada Near Corona de Tucson, Arizona. In *The Corona de Tucson Project, Prehistoric Use of a Bajada Environment,* by Bruce B. Huckell, Martyn D. Tagg, and Lisa W. Huckell, pp. 297–306. Archaeological Series No. 174. Arizona State Museum, Tucson.

Weaver, Donald E., Jr.
1974 *Archaeological Investigations at the Westwing Site, AZ T:7:27(ASM), Agua Fria River Valley, Arizona.* Anthropological Research Papers No. 7. Arizona State University, Tempe.

Whalen, Norman M.
1971 *Cochise Culture Sites in the Central San Pedro Drainage, Arizona.* Unpublished Ph.D. dissertation, Department of Anthropology, University of Arizona, Tucson.

128   *References*

Whiting, Alfred F.
   1939 *Ethnobotany of the Hopi*. Museum of Northern Arizona Bulletin No. 15. Flagstaff.

Wilson, Eldred D., Richard T. Moore, and H. Wesley Pierce
   1957 Geologic Map of Maricopa County, Arizona. Arizona Bureau of Mines, University of Arizona, Tucson.